Microwave Magic

Eggs and Cheese

Grolier Limited

TORONTO

Contributors to this series:

Recipes and Technical Assistance:
École de cuisine Bachand-Bissonnette
Cooking consultants:
Denis Bissonette
Michèle Émond
Dietician:
Christiane Barbeau
Photos:
Laramée Morel Communications
Audio-Visuelles
Design:
Claudette Taillefer
Assistants:
Julie Deslauriers
Philippe O'Connor
Joan Pothier
Accessories:
Andrée Cournoyer
Writing:
Communications La Griffe Inc.
Text Consultants:
Cap et bc inc.
Advisors:
Roger Aubin
Joseph R. De Varennes
Gaston Lavoie
Kenneth H. Pearson

Assembly:
Carole Garon
Vital Lapalme
Jean-Pierre Larose
Carl Simmons
Gus Soriano
Marc Vallières
Production Managers:
Gilles Chamberland
Ernest Homewood
Production Assistants:
Martine Gingras
Catherine Gordon
Kathy Kishimoto
Peter Thomlison
Art Director:
Bernard Lamy
Editors:
Laurielle Ilacqua
Susan Marshall
Margaret Oliver
Robin Rivers
Lois Rock
Jocelyn Smyth
Donna Thomson
Dolores Williams
Development:
Le Groupe Polygone Éditeurs Inc.

We wish to thank the following firms, PIER I IMPORTS and LE CACHE POT, for their contribution to the illustration of this set.

The series editors have taken every care to ensure that the information given is accurate. However, no cookbook can guarantee the user successful results. The editors cannot accept any responsibility for the results obtained by following the recipes and recommendations given.

Canadian Cataloguing in Publication Data

Main entry under title:

Eggs and cheese

(Microwave magic ; 16)
Translation of: Œufs et fromages.
Includes index.
ISBN 0-7172-2437-6

1. Cookery (Eggs). 2. Cookery (Cheese). 3. Microwave cookery. I. Series: Microwave magic (Toronto, Ont.) ; 16.

TX832.O4313 1988   641.6'75   C88-094215-0

Contents

Microwave Magic is a multi-volume set, with each volume devoted to a particular type of cooking. So, if you are looking for a chicken recipe, you simply go to one of the two volumes that deal with poultry. Each volume has its own index, and the final volume contains a general index to the complete set.

Microwave Magic puts over twelve hundred recipes at your fingertips. You will find it as useful as the microwave oven itself. Enjoy!

Note from the Editor

How to Use this Book
The books in this set have been designed to make your job as easy as possible. As a result, most of the recipes are set out in a standard way.

We suggest that you begin by consulting the information chart for the recipe you have chosen. You will find there all the information you need to decide if you are able to make it: preparation time, cost per serving, level of difficulty, number of calories per serving and other relevant details. Thus, if you have only 30 minutes in which to prepare the evening meal, you will quickly be able to tell which recipe is possible and suits your schedule.

The list of ingredients is always clearly separated from the main text. When space allows, the ingredients are shown together in a photograph so that you can make sure you have them all without rereading the list—

another way of saving your valuable time. In addition, for the more complex recipes we have supplied photographs of the key stages involved either in preparation or serving.

All the dishes in this book have been cooked in a 700 watt microwave oven. If your oven has a different wattage, consult the conversion chart that appears on the following page for cooking times in different types of oven. We would like to emphasize that the cooking times given in the book are a minimum. If a dish does not seem to be cooked enough, you may return it to the oven for a few more minutes. Also, the cooking time can vary according to your ingredients: their water and fat content, thickness, shape and even where they come from. We have therefore left a blank space on each recipe page in which you can note

the cooking time that suits you best. This will enable you to add a personal touch to the recipes that we suggest and to reproduce your best results every time.

Although we have put all the technical information together at the front of this book, we have inserted a number of boxed entries called **MICROTIPS** through-out to explain particular techniques. They are brief and simple, and will help you obtain successful results in your cooking.

With the very first recipe you try, you will discover just how simple microwave cooking can be and how often it depends on techniques you already use for cooking with a conventional oven. If cooking is a pleasure for you, as it is for us, it will be all the more so with a microwave oven. Now let's get on with the food.

The Editor

Key to the Symbols
For ease of reference, the following symbols have been used on the recipe information charts.

The pencil symbol is a reminder to write your cooking time in the space provided.

Level of Difficulty

Easy

Moderate

Complex

Cost per Serving

Inexpensive

Moderate

Expensive

Power Levels

All the recipes in this book have been tested in a 700 watt oven. As there are many microwave ovens on the market with different power levels, and as the names of these levels vary from one manufacturer to another, we have decided to give power levels as a percentage. To adapt the power levels given here, consult the chart opposite and the instruction manual for your oven.

Generally speaking, if you have a 500 watt or 600 watt oven you should increase cooking times by about 30% over those given, depending on the actual length of time required. The shorter the original cooking time, the greater the percentage by which it must be lengthened. The 30% figure is only an average. Consult the chart for detailed information on this topic.

Power Levels

HIGH: 100% - 90%	Vegetables (except boiled potatoes and carrots) Soup Sauce Fruits Browning ground beef Browning dish Popcorn
MEDIUM HIGH: 80% - 70%	Rapid defrosting of precooked dishes Muffins Some cakes Hot dogs
MEDIUM: 60% - 50%	Cooking tender meat Cakes Fish Seafood Eggs Reheating Boiled potatoes and carrots
MEDIUM LOW: 40%	Cooking less tender meat Simmering Melting chocolate
DEFROST: 30% **LOW: 30% - 20%**	Defrosting Simmering Cooking less tender meat
WARM: 10%	Keeping food warm Allowing yeast dough to rise

Cooking Time Conversion Chart

700 watts	600 watts*
5 s	11 s
15 s	20 s
30 s	40 s
45 s	1 min
1 min	1 min 20 s
2 min	2 min 40 s
3 min	4 min
4 min	5 min 20 s
5 min	6 min 40 s
6 min	8 min
7 min	9 min 20 s
8 min	10 min 40 s
9 min	12 min
10 min	13 min 30 s
20 min	26 min 40 s
30 min	40 min
40 min	53 min 40 s
50 min	66 min 40 s
1 h	1 h 20 min

* There is very little difference in cooking times between 500 watt ovens and 600 watt ovens.

Eggs and Cheese: A Source of Protein

Delicate, varied and nourishing, egg dishes as well as cheese dishes occupy a prominent place when good nourishment is considered.

Eggs, of course, are highly regarded by a large number of vegetarians; their high protein content makes them an excellent substitute for meat. Eggs are as highly regarded by gourmets with discriminating palates, diet-conscious diners and harried cooks because they form the basis of dishes that not only are delicious but low in calories and quick to prepare.

Eggs and cheese have many qualities in common. Both are rich in protein, an element essential to the body's formation of tissue. They are both practical foods: they can be kept for long periods of time and can be consumed as is, with no further preparation, if desired. Also, they form the basis of innumerable recipes. Often, an egg and/or cheese dish served with a green vegetable and with fruit for dessert will provide a satisfying and well-balanced meal.

On the following pages, we will discuss that most ancient source of protein in human history: the egg. The second part will deal with cheese, a food produced in all regions of the world, which has been greatly improved over the centuries by those pioneers in food chemistry—the cheese-makers.

Eggs: The Perfect Food

Geometricians and mathematicians have always considered the egg to be the perfect shape occurring in nature. Our perception of the egg, while not as poetic, is equally valid: the egg is a storehouse of precious proteins. In fact, two eggs are equivalent to 60 to 90 grams (2 to 3 ounces) of meat, fish or poultry. Furthermore, eggs provide all the known vitamins with the exception of Vitamin C and one egg has only 80 calories. This, of course, is a very important consideration to most people on diets. Eggs are a very versatile food; they are used to impart a lightness to soufflés, pastry and cakes, to thicken mayonnaise and sauces and to give a pleasing golden color to foods cooked in the oven. Not surprisingly, every Canadian consumes close to 18 dozen eggs per year, on their own, in other dishes or in packaged foods.

If your cholesterol levels are too high, you need not give up eggs altogether: simply cut in half the amount of egg yolks required in a recipe.

Do you live alone? Do you hate to spend hours trapped in your kitchen? Perhaps you're simply looking for a bit of creativity in your diet. Then, forget about the ho-hum ham sandwich with mayonnaise and think about eggs. Your appetite will come out of its shell!

Eggs in the Microwave: A Simple Operation

Eggs are a fragile food and are very sensitive to heat. The cooking of eggs requires care and precision, especially in the microwave oven where the cooking is very rapid. With a microwave oven, the cooking time will vary depending on the kind of egg used and also on the quantity. Furthermore, the very make-up of the egg demands extra precautions: with traditional cooking methods, the white will start to cook before the yolk; the opposite is true in the microwave oven; the microwaves are attracted to the fat contained in the yolk which will be cooked before the whites can be cooked.

Anyone watching his or her diet will prefer eggs done in the microwave oven, as less fat is required than with conventional cooking methods. In effect, the heat from a regular stove partially breaks down the fats contained in butter, for example. The speed of microwave cooking eliminates this action and requires much less fat.

With a toothpick, pierce the membrane that covers the yolk to allow heat to escape during cooking. Otherwise, the yolk might explode during cooking and you will have a clean-up job to do in your oven.

The microwave oven offers a variety of cooking methods. Eggs can, in effect, be baked, poached, scrambled or made into omelettes in a very few minutes, sometimes in seconds and without fat. There is one aspect, however, that has not changed with the advent of the microwave oven: the cooking of egg dishes such as custards and sauces requires precision. A slight miscalculation and you'll find yourself with a mass of lumps or containers that must be scoured because food has stuck to them.

Before cooking an egg, make sure you gently pierce the membrane that covers the yolk with a toothpick. This simple trick will prevent the yolk from exploding. It is also wise to pierce the white in two or three places.

When cooking eggs, remember that it is preferable to remove them before they look quite done. As with other foods, the eggs will continue to cook after being removed from the microwave oven.

Above all, remember this golden rule of culinary art: it is always easier to return a dish to the oven than to try to rescue an overcooked one.

Wanted: Fresh Eggs

Are your eggs fresh? There is a way to check them without cracking them open. An egg has a porous shell and the water which encloses the inner part of the egg evaporates and the air chamber becomes larger as the egg becomes older. To check the freshness of an egg, shake it gently near your ear. If you feel the contents moving about inside the shell, it's fairly certain the egg was not laid recently! An equally efficient test is to plunge an egg in water. An older egg has a larger air chamber and is therefore lighter and will float. A fresh egg is heavy and will sink to the bottom of the bowl of water. If it is a few days old, it will have a tendency to float vertically in the water; and if it is two to three weeks old, it will float near the surface. If it floats on top of the water, it would be best not to use it at all for cooking.

A fresh egg, cracked open, has a round yolk, well centered and surrounded by a thick milky liquid, and the exterior membrane is quite thin. As an egg gets older, the white becomes clearer and the yolk moves away from the center. A stale egg is abnormally liquid when broken open.

These different ways of testing for freshness are very effective. They are more reliable than some more or less credible methods that should be ignored, one of which is to judge freshness by the color of the yolk. A dark

Does the egg sink to the bottom? That means it's a very fresh egg! If it has a tendency to float to the surface, its air chamber is fairly large, indicating it has lost some of its freshness.

yolk does not indicate an old egg! In fact, a freshly laid egg might have a very dark yolk: its color usually depends on the type of chicken and on the feed being used. Don't let yourself be guided strictly by the color of an egg in determining its freshness. Remember too, that the egg is a very fragile food: an hour on the counter of a warm kitchen is equivalent to the loss of one day's freshness. It is therefore important to take

precautions to preserve eggs at their best. You will find, on page 15 of this volume, some easy-to-follow directions on how to store your eggs. Even if you insist on extra fresh eggs, you can make use of those that don't quite meet your standard: use them for facial masks, skin treatments, etc. Recipes for such preparations can be found in many health and beauty books dealing with natural plants and foods.

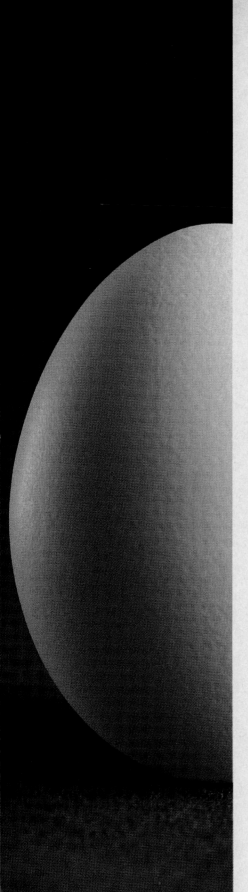

All Kinds of Eggs

Scrambled Eggs

Scrambled eggs and the microwave oven have proved to be very compatible. The white and the yolk, mixed together, produce a homogeneous mixture of elements that react equally to the microwaves and cook extremely well. Without fat, mixed with milk (skim or otherwise) or even with water (which will make them lighter), scrambled eggs cook even better in a microwave oven than with conventional methods. Into a bowl or a large measuring cup, crack two eggs and add 30 mL (2 tablespoons) of liquid. Season the mixture to taste and whip. Cook at 100% for 1-1/2 minutes, stirring every 30 seconds. The eggs should not look completely cooked when removed from the oven. Break the cooked eggs up with a fork and serve. If your oven does not have a mechanism to distribute the microwaves evenly or a turntable, give the cooking dish a half-turn halfway through the cooking time.

Poached Eggs

Place 250 mL (1 cup) boiling water, 5 mL (1 teaspoon) white or cider vinegar and a pinch of salt in a round 500 mL (2 cup) dish that is microwave safe. The vinegar helps to set the egg white.

One at a time, break two eggs, at room temperature, into the cooking dish. Gently pierce each yolk and white in 2 or 3 places with a toothpick. Cover and cook at 100% for 1 to 1-1/2 minutes. Allow the eggs to sit in the water for 1 to 2 minutes and then drain before serving. Make sure not to overcook as the egg yolks might explode.

Shirred Eggs

In a well-greased ramekin, melt 1 to 2 mL (1/4 to 1/2 teaspoon) butter for 25 seconds. Break an egg into the butter and, without breaking the yolk, pierce it and the white in two or three places with a toothpick. Cook at 70% for 35 to 40 seconds for each egg or just until the whites begin to set. You will perhaps hear a crackling sound during the cooking; it is nothing to worry about if you have pierced the yolks. Remove the eggs from the oven before they seem completely cooked; the cooking process will continue even after their removal from the oven. If your oven does not have a mechanism that distributes the microwaves or a turntable, give the cooking dish a half-turn halfway through the cooking time.

Omelettes

There are two kinds of omelette: an ordinary, basic one and a soufflé omelette. Basic omelettes are rolled, stuffed or garnished, and are usually served as an entrée or main course. The soufflé omelette resembles that elegant concoction baked in the oven in a special dish with straight sides but is more simply baked in a long dish and served as an hors d'oeuvres or a hot, sweet side dish.

Basic Omelette

In a pie plate, melt 30 mL (2 tablespoons) butter and spread it evenly over the plate. In a bowl, whisk 3 eggs and pour them gently into the greased plate. Place on a raised rack and cook at 70% for 2 to 3 minutes, stirring once. Garnish the omelette with cheese, cooked vegetables or ham, if desired.

Soufflé Omelette

Beat egg whites into peaks (a maximum of 4 eggs) and add the yolks, also beaten. If you want an entrée or side dish that is seasoned, add some "fine herbs" and cook the mixture as you would a basic omelette. For a sweet dessert omelette that resembles a soufflé, sprinkle the mixture with sugar before putting it in the oven.

Soufflé

Beat 6 egg whites into peaks, and add 7 mL (1-1/2 teaspoons) cream of tartar. Beat the egg yolks with same beaters mixing in 500 mL (2 cups) cheese sauce. Gently fold the cheese mixture into the beaten egg whites, stirring just enough to distribute it evenly. Pour the mixture into a soufflé dish and cook at 50% for 15 to 20 minutes. Serve immediately. As well as cooking very quickly, a soufflé cooked in a microwave oven rises a lot because no crust forms to keep it down. You must, therefore, use a larger dish than usual. The soufflé is cooked when the top of it appears to be dry.

Quiche

Brush a pie crust with an egg yolk mixed with 5 mL (1 teaspoon) Worcestershire sauce. Sprinkle the crust with bits of bacon and grated cheese. Pour in a mixture made by beating 3 eggs, 125 mL (1/2 cup) 35% cream, salt and pepper. Place on a raised rack and cook at 70% for 10 to 12 minutes. Allow to stand for a short time before serving.

Shopping and Storage Guide for Eggs

White shells or brown shells? The debate that surrounds this question is pointless since the color of the shells is determined solely by the kind of chicken that lays it. White or brown, the eggs have the same nutritional value and the same taste. The controversy over the color of the yolks is equally pointless: a pale yellow yolk means the chicken was raised on wheat; a darker yolk means it was fed corn or that the poultry farmer added some coloring to the mash fed to the chicken. In short, the color of the yolk has nothing to do with its nutritional value.

The Classification of Eggs

Eggs sold in supermarkets have been inspected and graded according to standards set by Agriculture Canada. Most eggs are Grade A1. Some stores will carry eggs classified as Grade A. These eggs are no different, with respect to nutrition from those classed A1; only their appearance is different. The classifications B and C are generally destined for the food industry.

Always choose eggs that are clean and unbroken. Be careful with any cracked eggs you may find; use them in cooking to make sure they don't contain salmonella, a bacteria that may penetrate cracked eggs. Traces of blood or a slight greenish tinge to the egg white (which is a sign of a strong proportion of riboflavin—Vitamin B_2) do not in any way affect the quality of the egg.

Categories of Eggs

Category A   produced by chickens that have been laying for 2 to 6 months and sold within one week of being laid;
yolk is firm and well-centered;
white is thick;
air chamber is very small.

Category B   yolk is somewhat off-center;
white is more watery;
air chamber is larger.

Extra large	765 g (27 oz) / dozen
Large	680 g (24 oz) / dozen
Medium	595 g (21 oz) / dozen
Small	510 g (18 oz) / dozen
Pee wee	less than 510 g (18 oz) / dozen

MICROTIPS

Eggs at Room Temperature
It is always preferable to use eggs at room temperature. Egg whites allowed to stand for 30 minutes at room temperature, for example, will result in a greater volume when beaten than if beaten directly upon removal from the refrigerator.

Storage of Eggs

As soon as you get home, place the eggs in the warmest part of the refrigerator. Make sure they are not placed next to foods with a strong odor. Because the shell is very porous, your eggs could pick up odors that would alter their taste. The box the eggs are sold in is really the perfect container. If, however, you wish to transfer them to the egg holder in your refrigerator, do so carefully, with the pointed end down as they are placed in the egg box. Placing them in this manner avoids compressing the air chamber and keeps the egg yolk in its place. Eggs can be stored in the refrigerator for 1 month.

MICROTIPS

Beware of Cooking Eggs in Their Shells

Never try to cook an egg in its shell in the microwave oven. The effect of the heat on the egg inside the shell would be to increase the pressure and cause it to explode in a very few minutes. The mess in your oven would be considerable. Never try to reheat hard-cooked eggs in the microwave. Slice them or cut them in half and cover them with a sauce to prevent them from drying out.

Preventing Yolks From Getting Hard

To store egg yolks in the refrigerator, cover with a little water or milk to prevent hardening. They will keep in this manner for four days. The whites will keep in a covered container for two to three days.

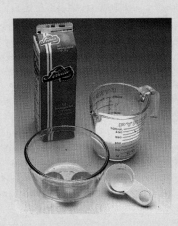

Cheeses

Chance, we are told, played a big part in the discovery of cheese. Many centuries ago, a shepherd was carrying milk in a goatskin. It was fresh in the morning, but by evening, the heat had curdled the milk into the world's first cheese: the ancestor of hundreds of cheeses enjoyed around the world today. From a mild cheddar with its delicious taste of fresh milk, to a pungent Roquefort covered with blue mold, to a soft runny Camembert, cheeses come in so many varieties (more than 400 in France) that there has to be one with the flavor and texture you like. Cheese is a healthy food as well as a delicious one; it contains protein and most of the nutrients found in milk (proteins, calcium, phosphorous and vitamins).

An all purpose food, cheese can be used in appetizers, as the mainstay of a meal or perhaps as a snack at the end of an evening; cheese is often used as a base for dips or to accompany a glass of good wine after the theater. Even without cooking, cheese plays an important role in the kitchen. Onion soup, Italian dishes and many sauces are much improved by the addition of some grated cheese. The French word for cheese is *fromage,* drawn from the Greek word *formos* and the Latin *forma,* meaning the form or mold used to drain the curds and shape the cheese. There is a whole lexicon of words devoted to cheese. For example, certain cheeses, such as Port-Salut and Parmesan, are said to be "ripe" after they have been left to mature in cellars for a certain number of days or weeks, perhaps even years, before going to market. Other cheeses, such as cottage cheese or cream cheese, are not fermented and are said to be "fresh." Cheeses are usually classed by the degree of moisture they contain. Cheese with a moisture content over 50% is considered a soft cheese; in this group, you would find Brie, Camembert and other cheeses that are spreadable. If they contain less than 50% moisture, such as Swiss, Gouda or Emmenthal, we call them "hard" cheeses. Soft or hard? It's your choice!

Soft Cheeses

Soft cheeses are made by the slow drainage of raw curds. Their moisture content can go as high as 75% in the case of double-cream cheese, for example. Many varieties of soft cheeses are available in the markets today. Most of them originated in Europe but our master cheese-makers have developed their own varieties that are equally as good. In cheese spreads or served with crackers, soft cheeses, such as fresh spicy goat's milk cheese, are delicious. Many of them can serve as a base for dips. Whether eaten as is or made into a spread, soft cheeses are varied and delicious. Here are a few of the soft cheeses:

1. Cream cheese
2. Cream cheese rolled in "fine herbs"
3. Kirsch-flavored cheese
4. Saint-André
5. Saint-Paulin
6. Belle crème
7. Baron au poivre
8. Blue cheese
9. Pepper cream cheese
10. Camembert
11. Brie
12. Oka
13. Goat's milk cheese
14. Double cream

Hard Cheeses

Whether it is a Canadian cheddar, known the world over, a Munster, perhaps flavored with cumin, a Gouda, all wrapped up in its red wax or its twin Edam, made from skim milk, a Jarlsberg, full of holes or perhaps a Gruyère, the number one ingredient of fondues and quiches—one will always find a hard cheese on the shopping list of health-conscious individuals. Trying out the many varieties is like leaving on a long trip around the world.

Here is a list of the more popular hard cheeses:

1. Tilsit
2. Jarlsberg
3. Emmenthal
4. Mild orange cheddar
5. Black Forest
6. Friulano
7. Parmesan
8. Farmer
9. Limburger
10. Mozzarella
11. Medium cheddar
12. Brick
13. Smoked Gouda
14. Provolone
15. Dutch Edam
16. Havarti
17. Swiss Gruyère
18. Munster
19. Colby

A Few Words On Some of the Great Cheeses

Each cheese found in the market is the result of long years of research and trial and error. Some types appear regularly on our tables, others only rarely. The following is a brief catalogue of some of the better cheeses. You've probably heard the names but have you ever tasted them . . . ?

The *Baron au poivre* is a Canadian cheese, round and flat, the same type of cheese as Oka and Port-Salut. *Brick* cheese, an American creation, is a hard cheese that slices well; it is very similar to cheddar. Soft cheeses encased in their own crust, such as *Brie* and *Camembert,* should be eaten soon after they are purchased and are usually bought in small quantities. Mild *cheddar* cheese has a delicate flavor that becomes increasingly sharp as it ripens and dries. Canada has long been noted for its production of quality cheddar cheese. *Goat's milk* cheese is a fresh cheese with a flavor that is piquant and salty. *Colby* cheese is a variety of cheddar that is milder, softer and easier to slice. Double-cream and triple-cream cheeses contain very high levels of fat (up to 75%) which give them a delicate, buttery taste. A mild Dutch cheese, *Edam* is made with partially skimmed milk and is protected with a layer of red wax. *Emmenthal,* of Swiss origin, is a hard cheese with many holes in it. *Feta* cheese is a white cheese which has been soaked in brine, imported from Greece. It is used in the preparation of Greek salads. *Gorgonzola* is an Italian blue cheese. *Gouda* closely resembles Edam, except that it is made from skim milk instead of partially skimmed. *Gruyère* cheese is Swiss in origin; it is somewhat drier than Emmenthal and is used in the preparation of Quiche Lorraine and onion soup au gratin. *Havarti* is the Danish equivalent of Tilsit cheese. *Jarlsberg* is a Norwegian cheese sold in rounds with an oily texture and full of holes. *Monterey Jack* is a hard cheese which was developed in Monterey, a region in California. Soft and spongy, with a delicate flavor, *mozzarella* is an important ingredient in many Italian dishes. *Munster* is a semi-hard but creamy cheese sometimes flavored with cumin or anise.

Cooking Cheese

Parmesan is one of the better known hard Italian cheeses. Strong and aromatic, it is a fine table cheese but is also excellent for use in the kitchen. *Provolone* is a hard Italian cheese with a yellow crust and a creamy white color. *Raclette,* originating in Switzerland, has the same name as the dish in which it is the main ingredient—a type of cheese fondue prepared at the table and served over boiled potatoes with onions and pickled gherkins. A milk Italian cheese, crumbly and dry, *Ricotta* is very low in fat. It is used mostly for cooking. *Romano* is an Italian cheese made from ewe's milk and often used in grated form. A milk cheese, *Rondelé,* is usually flavored with garlic and fine herbs and used as hors d'oeuvres, canapés or as a garnish on baked potatoes. *Saint-Paulin* is a semi-hard cheese with an orange crust. *Tomme au raisin* is a Gruyère-like cream cheese—a process cheese that once was covered with the residue from wine-making, the marc of the grapes. *Tilsit* is a German cheese, semi-hard with irregular openings in its texture.

Cheese, rich in fats, cooks very quickly in the microwave oven. You must be very careful with your timing as cheese that is overcooked becomes tough, rubbery and indigestible. If your oven is not equipped with a mechanism to distribute microwaves evenly or a rotating turntable, make sure you turn the dish during the cooking process. Whenever possible, add the cheese at the end of the cooking period and remove the dish as soon as the cheese starts to melt.

Two important rules:
1. It is always easier to return a dish to the oven for a minute or two longer than it is to try to rescue a dish that has been overcooked.

2. If your oven does not automatically distribute the microwaves evenly or does not have a turntable, make sure you rotate the dish during the cooking period.

MICROTIPS

How To Serve Cheese

Cheeses are much softer and more flavorful when served at room temperature. Remove them for the refrigerator at least an hour before serving or warm them at 30% for about 1 minute in the microwave oven.

Storage of Cheese

Cheese is best kept in a cool, dry spot. Place it in the warmest part of the refrigerator—in the vegetable crisper, for instance. Cheeses keep very well in their original packaging or they can be sealed hermetically with plastic wrap or aluminum foil. Soft cheeses will keep for about one week, while hard cheeses will keep for up to 6 weeks.

Omelette Country Style

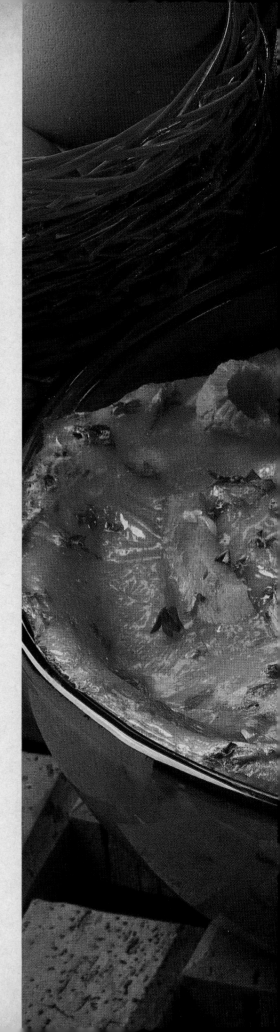

Level of Difficulty	🍴
Preparation Time	10 min
Cost per Serving	$
Number of Servings	2
Nutritional Value	270 calories 20.5 g protein 54.8 mg iron
Food Exchanges	3 oz meat 1 fat exchange
Cooking Time	4 min*
Standing Time	2 min
Power Level	100%, 70%
Write Your Cooking Time Here	

* Cooking time is based on the use of large eggs which are at room temperature when cooking begins.

Ingredients
4 large eggs
50 mL (1/4 cup) milk
salt and pepper to taste
15 mL (1 tablespoon) parsley
50 mL (1/4 cup) ham, cut into fine strips
10 mL (2 teaspoons) butter

Method
— Whisk the eggs, milk, salt, pepper and parsley together; add the ham and set aside.
— Place the butter in a microwave-safe pie plate and heat at 100% for 30 seconds or until melted.
— Swirl the butter over the entire surface of the pie plate and pour in the egg mixture.
— Place the plate on a raised rack in the oven and cook at 70% for 1 minute.
— With a fork, move the uncooked egg mixture from the center to the edges and continue cooking at 70% for 2 to 3 minutes or until the omelette is cooked.
— Let stand for 2 minutes.

Omelette Provençale

Level of Difficulty	🍴🍴
Preparation Time	15 min
Cost per Serving	$
Number of Servings	4
Nutritional Value	254 calories 15.4 g protein 3.1 mg iron
Food Exchanges	2 oz meat 2 fat exchanges
Cooking Time	7 min*
Standing Time	2 min
Power Level	70%
Write Your Cooking Time Here	

* Cooking time is based on the use of large eggs which are at room
temperature when cooking begins.

MICROTIPS

Beating Egg Whites

Before beating the egg whites, heat them in the microwave at 100% for 5 to 10 seconds per egg white. Don't worry if the edges appear to cook a little; this won't matter as long as you beat the egg whites as soon as you remove them from the oven. Warmed up in this manner, the egg whites will produce a stiff meringue.

Ingredients
8 large eggs
90 g (3 oz) anchovy fillets, cut lengthwise
2 cloves garlic
15 mL (1 tablespoon) oil
15 mL (1 tablespoon) soft butter
15 mL (1 tablespoon) parsley
5 mL (1 teaspoon) lemon juice
pepper to taste
black olives, cut in pieces, to taste

Method
— Beat the eggs lightly; set aside.
— Chop half the anchovies finely and set them aside.
— With a garlic press, crush the garlic cloves; add the oil and soft butter, and mix to a smooth paste. Combine with the chopped anchovies.
— Add the parsley, lemon juice and pepper; mix well and stir into the beaten eggs.
— Spray the inside of a 22.5 cm (9 inch) pie plate with an anti-stick coating, such as Pam, and pour in the mixture.
— Place the plate on a raised rack in the oven and cook at 70% for 2 minutes.
— With a fork, move the uncooked egg mixture from the center to the edges and continue cooking at 70% for 2 to 3 minutes or until the omelette is cooked to your taste.
— Let stand for 2 minutes and garnish with the remaining whole anchovy fillets.
— If you wish, sprinkle pieces of black olives over the omelette before serving.

Zucchini Omelette

Level of Difficulty	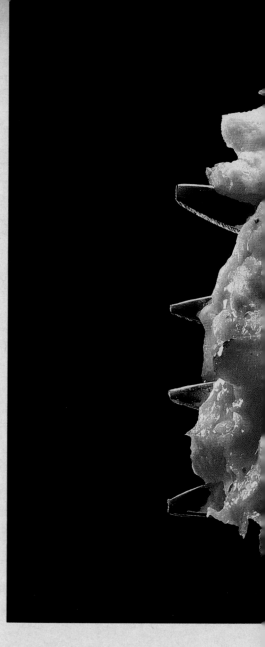
Preparation Time	20 min
Cost per Serving	$
Number of Servings	3
Nutritional Value	220 calories 15 g protein 223 mg iron
Food Exchanges	2 oz meat 1 vegetable exchange 1/2 bread exchange
Cooking Time	5 min*
Standing Time	2 min
Power Level	70%
Write Your Cooking Time Here	

* Cooking time is based on the use of large eggs which are at room temperature when cooking begins.

Ingredients
4 large eggs
6 small zucchinis
1 clove garlic, chopped
50 mL (1/4 cup) Parmesan cheese, grated
50 mL (1/4 cup) flour
salt and pepper to taste
5 mL (1 teaspoon) butter

Method
— Grate the zucchini coarsely; wrap in a clean cloth and press with your hands to squeeze out as much water as possible.
— Break the eggs into a bowl and beat with a fork; add the grated zucchini, garlic and Parmesan cheese.
— Gradually add the flour, stirring constantly; season to taste.
— Grease a microwave-safe pie plate with butter and pour in the egg mixture.
— Place the plate on a raised rack and cook at 70% for 3 to 5 minutes, stirring once after 2 minutes of cooking.
— Let stand for 2 minutes.

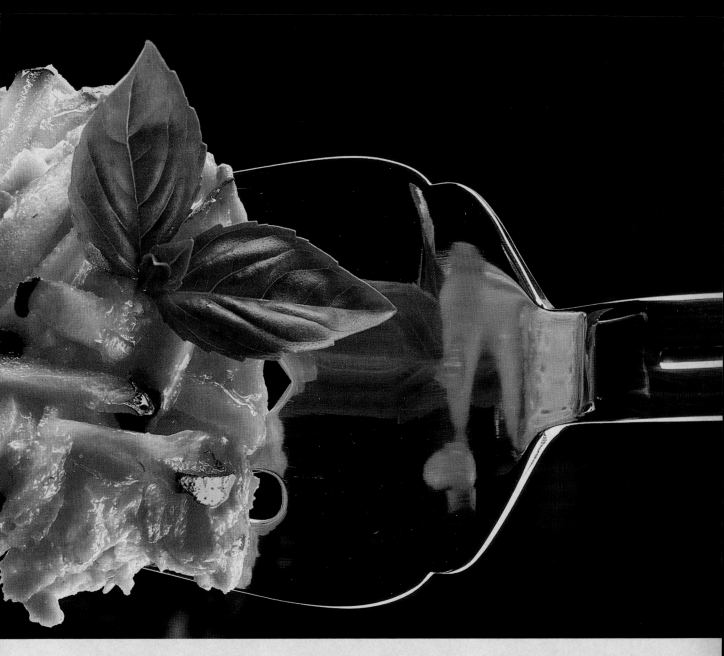

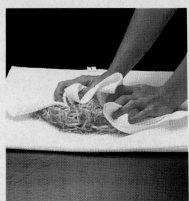

Simple and quick to prepare, this omelette with zucchini calls for the ingredients assembled here.

Wrap the grated zucchini in a clean cloth and press to extract as much water as possible.

Pour the egg mixture into a buttered pie plate and place on a raised rack in the oven.

Springtime Omelette

Level of Difficulty	🍴
Preparation Time	15 min
Cost per Serving	**$**
Number of Servings	4
Nutritional Value	235 calories 22.5 g protein 135 mg iron
Food Exchanges	2.5 oz meat 2 vegetable exchanges
Cooking Time	15 min*
Standing Time	2 min
Power Level	100%, 70%
Write Your Cooking Time Here	

* Cooking time is based on the use of large eggs which are at room temperature when cooking begins.

Ingredients
6 large eggs
450 g (1 lb) fresh asparagus
30 mL (2 tablespoons) water
250 mL (1 cup) cottage cheese
salt and pepper to taste
250 mL (1 cup) mushrooms, sliced
6 slices tomato
30 mL (2 tablespoons) Parmesan cheese, grated

Method
— Place the asparagus in a dish with the water; cover and cook at 100% for 4 to 6 minutes, giving the dish a half-turn halfway through the cooking time.
— Remove the asparagus from the oven and drain; set 4 asparagus spears aside and cut the others in three pieces; set aside.
— Break the eggs into a bowl and beat with a fork, gradually adding the cottage cheese, salt and pepper; add the asparagus pieces and the mushrooms.
— Spray the inside of a 25 cm (10 inch), microwave-safe pie plate with a non-stick coating and pour in the egg mixture.
— Cover the plate and place on a raised rack in the oven; cook at 70% for 6 to 8 minutes, giving the plate a half-turn halfway through the cooking time.
— Garnish with the remaining asparagus spears and tomato slices, and sprinkle with Parmesan cheese.
— Increase the power to 100% and cook for 1 minute.
— Let stand for 2 minutes.

Here are the ingredients required to make this springtime omelette—a dish that is quick to prepare and pleases everyone.

Cook the asparagus in a dish with 30 mL (2 tablespoons) water.

Coat the inside of a pie plate with a non-stick spray.

Monday Omelette

Level of Difficulty	🍴
Preparation Time	15 min
Cost per Serving	$
Number of Servings	4
Nutritional Value	288 calories 17.5 g protein 162 mg iron
Food Exchanges	2.5 oz meat 1/2 vegetable exchange 2 fat exchanges
Cooking Time	7 min*
Standing Time	2 min
Power Level	70%, 100%
Write Your Cooking Time Here	

* Cooking time is based on the use of large eggs which are at room temperature when cooking begins.

Ingredients
6 large eggs
50 mL (1/4 cup) 35% cream
50 mL (1/4 cup) green peas
50 mL (1/4 cup) carrots, diced
125 mL (1/2 cup) ham, cut into cubes
salt and pepper to taste
125 mL (1/2 cup) orange cheddar cheese, grated

Method
— Break the eggs in a bowl and beat with a whisk, gradually adding the cream.
— Stir in the vegetables and ham; season to taste.
— Spray the inside of a 22.5 cm (9 inch) pie plate with a non-stick coating and pour in the mixture.
— Place the pie plate on a raised rack and cook at 70% for 4 to 6 minutes, stirring after 2 minutes of cooking.
— Sprinkle with the grated cheese and continue cooking at 100% for 1 minute.
— Cover and allow to stand for 2 minutes before serving.

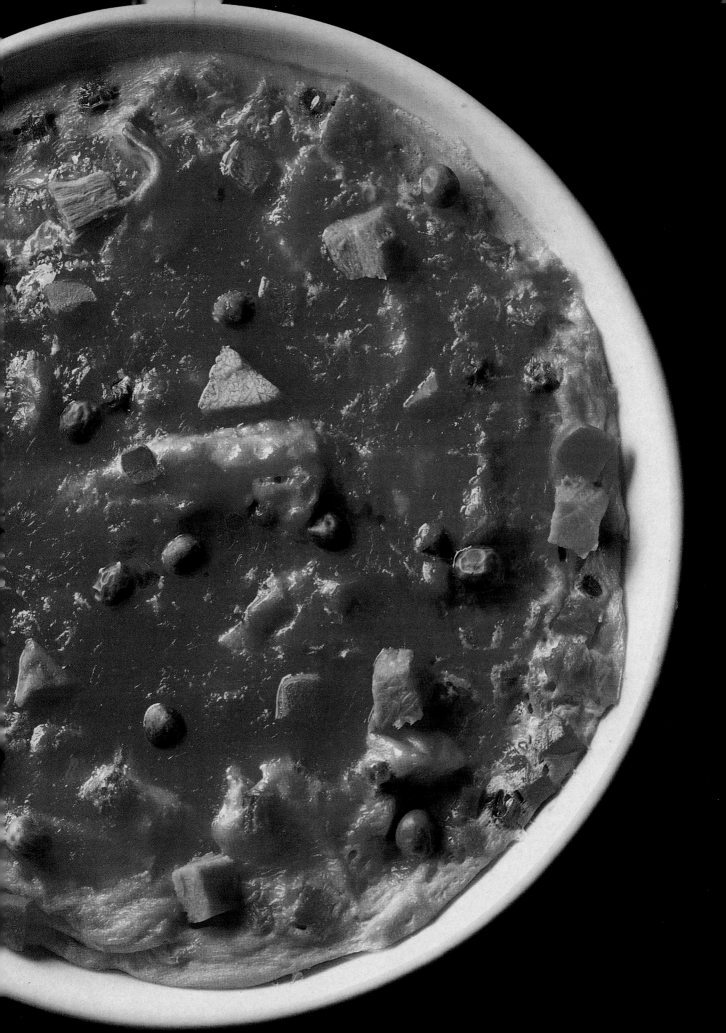

Spanish Omelette

Level of Difficulty	🍴🍴
Preparation Time	20 min
Cost per Serving	$
Number of Servings	6
Nutritional Value	390 calories 21.9 g protein 3.4 mg iron
Food Exchanges	3.5 oz meat 1 vegetable exchange 2 fat exchanges
Cooking Time	20 min*
Standing Time	5 min
Power Level	90%, 100%, 70%
Write Your Cooking Time Here	

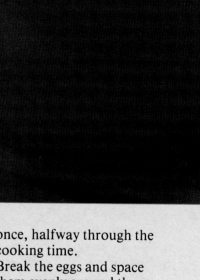

* Cooking time is based on the use of large eggs which are at room temperature when cooking begins.

Ingredients
6 large eggs
225 g (8 oz) Italian sausage, sliced thinly
1 small onion, chopped finely
2 garlic cloves, chopped finely
1 red pepper, peeled, chopped and drained
225 g (8 oz) Italian ham, diced
15 mL (1 tablespoon) tomato paste
pinch of thyme
2 mL (1/2 teaspoon) oregano
salt and pepper to taste
15 mL (1 tablespoon) parsley

Method
— Place the sausage slices on a bacon rack and cook at 90% for 2 to 3 minutes, giving the dish a half-turn halfway through the cooking time. Set aside.
— Put the onion, garlic and red pepper in a dish; cover and cook at 100% for 3 minutes.
— Add the cooked sausage and all the remaining ingredients except the eggs.
— Cover and cook at 100% for 7 to 9 minutes, stirring once, halfway through the cooking time.
— Break the eggs and space them evenly around the outside edge of the dish.
— Place the dish on a raised rack in the oven and cook, uncovered, at 100% for 1 minute.
— Reduce the power to 70% and cook 3 to 4 minutes, giving the dish a half-turn halfway through the cooking time.
— Let stand for 5 minutes.

Assemble all these ingredients and in less than an hour, you will have an omelette that will be a joy to serve to your guests.

Place slices of sausage on a bacon rack and cook them. Give the rack a half-turn halfway through the cooking time.

Break the eggs and space evenly around the outside edge of the dish.

Salmon Omelette

Level of Difficulty	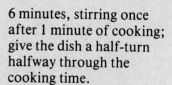
Preparation Time	10 min
Cost per Serving	$
Number of Servings	4
Nutritional Value	161 calories 16.8 g protein 1.6 mg iron
Food Exchanges	2 oz meat
Cooking Time	8 min*
Standing Time	2 min
Power Level	70%
Write Your Cooking Time Here	

* Cooking time is based on the use of large eggs which are at room temperature when cooking begins.

Ingredients
4 large eggs
45 mL (3 tablespoons) milk
salt and pepper to taste
125 mL (1/2 cup) salmon
4 green onions, finely chopped
2 mL (1/2 teaspoon) dill

Method
— Separate the whites and yolks of the eggs; beat the whites until stiff peaks form and set aside.
— Beat the yolks and gradually add the milk; season to taste.
— Gently fold the egg whites into the yolk mixture.
— Spray the inside of a pie plate with a non-stick coating and pour in the mixture.
— Place the pie plate on a raised rack in the oven and cook at 70% for 5 to 6 minutes, stirring once after 1 minute of cooking; give the dish a half-turn halfway through the cooking time.
— Allow to stand for 2 minutes.
— Meanwhile, combine the salmon, green onions and dill in a bowl; mix well.
— Cook at 100% for 2 minutes, stirring once.
— Cover the cooked omelette with the salmon mixture and fold it over before serving.

Assemble these few ingredients before preparing this salmon omelette.

Beat the egg whites until they form stiff peaks.

After cooking the omelette, cover it with the mixture of salmon, green onions and dill.

37

Apple Omelette Flambé

Level of Difficulty	🍴🍴
Preparation Time	15 min
Cost per Serving	$ $
Number of Servings	2
Nutritional Value	420 calories 12 g protein 2.6 mg iron
Food Exchanges	2 oz meat 2-1/2 fruit exchanges 2-1/2 fat exchanges
Cooking Time	8 min*
Standing Time	1 min
Power Level	100%, 70%
Write Your Cooking Time Here	

MICROTIPS

How To Prepare a Perfect Omelette

If the omelette appears too runny, return it to the oven for another 30 seconds. However, be careful not to overcook it and remember that the omelette will continue to cook even after being removed from the oven.

* Cooking time is based on the use of large eggs which are at room temperature when cooking begins.

Ingredients
4 large eggs
2 apples
30 mL (2 tablespoons) butter
50 mL (1/4 cup) icing sugar
salt

Garnish:
30 mL (2 tablespoons) icing sugar
30 mL (2 tablespoons) calvados

Method
— Peel the apples, core them and cut into thin slices.
— Melt the butter in a dish at 100% for 30 seconds.
— Place the apple slices in the dish, cover and cook at 100% for 1-1/2 to 2 minutes.
— Sprinkle with 50 mL (1/4 cup) icing sugar, replace the cover and set aside.
— In a bowl, beat the eggs, adding a pinch of salt.
— Spray the inside of a 20 cm (8 inch) pie plate with a non-stick coating and pour in the eggs.
— Place the pie plate on a raised rack and cook at 70% for 3 to 4 minutes, stirring once after 2 minutes of cooking; give the plate a half-turn halfway through the cooking time.
— Allow to stand for 1 minute then lay the apple slices over the surface of the omelette.
— Sprinkle with the remaining icing sugar and set aside.
— Heat the calvados at 100% for 30 seconds; pour over the omelette and light with a flame; serve immediately.

Fruit Omelette

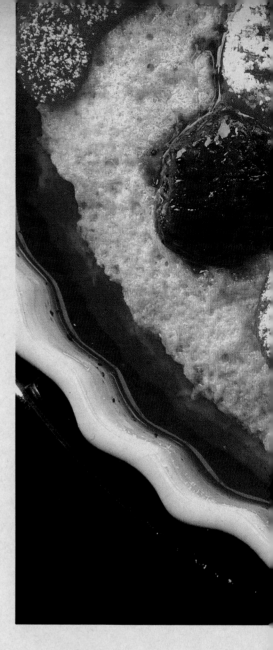

Level of Difficulty	🍴
Preparation Time	20 min
Cost per Serving	$
Number of Servings	4
Nutritional Value	213 calories 10.3 g protein 2.4 mg iron
Food Exchanges	1.5 oz meat 1-1/2 fruit exchanges
Cooking Time	8 min*
Standing Time	2 min
Power Level	70%, 100%
Write Your Cooking Time Here	

* Cooking time is based on the use of large eggs which are at room temperature when cooking begins.

Ingredients
6 large eggs
2 mL (1/2 teaspoon) baking powder
75 mL (1/3 cup) milk
2 mL (1/2 teaspoon) salt
pinch of pepper
1 284 g (10 oz) package frozen strawberries
10 mL (2 teaspoons) cornstarch
225 g (8 oz) mandarin orange sections, well drained
30 mL (2 tablespoons) icing sugar

Method
— Separate the whites and yolks of the eggs; beat the egg whites until they form stiff peaks; set aside.
— Beat the egg yolks, gradually adding the baking powder, milk, salt and pepper.
— Gently fold the egg whites into the yolk mixture.
— Spray the inside of a 22.5 cm (9 inch) pie plate with a non-stick coating, such as Pam, and pour in the egg mixture.
— Place the pie plate on a raised rack and cook at 70% for 4 to 5 minutes, stirring after 2 minutes of cooking.
— Drain the strawberries in a strainer and set the juice aside.
— In a small bowl, dissolve the cornstarch in the strawberry juice; cook at 100% for 2 to 3 minutes or until the mixture thickens, stirring twice during the cooking time.
— Add the strawberries and the mandarin orange sections to the sauce and mix.
— Pour this fruit mixture over the omelette and sprinkle with icing sugar before serving.

Here are the ingredients you will need to produce this flavorful omelette in just 30 minutes.

Spray the inside of a pie plate with a non-stick coating before pouring in the egg mixture.

Eggs Benedict

Level of Difficulty	🍴🍴
Preparation Time	15 min
Cost per Serving	**$**
Number of Servings	6
Nutritional Value	515 calories 19.1 g protein 3.7 mg iron
Food Exchanges	2 oz meat 2 bread exchanges 4-1/2 fat exchanges
Cooking Time	16 min*
Standing Time	None
Power Level	100%
Write Your Cooking Time Here	

* Cooking time is based on the use of large eggs which are at room temperature when cooking begins.

Ingredients
6 large eggs
1.5 L (6 cups) water
50 mL (1/4 cup) white vinegar
3 English muffins, cut in half and toasted
6 slices cooked ham
1 recipe hot Hollandaise Sauce (see recipe on page 12 of *Sauces and Soups*, Volume 11)

Method
— First, prepare the Hollandaise Sauce; set aside and keep warm.
— Pour the water and vinegar into a dish; cover and bring to a boil by heating at 100% for 10 to 12 minutes.
— Meanwhile, break the eggs into a pie plate, taking care not to break the yolks.
— Very gently, slide the eggs

⇒

42

Eggs Benedict

Poached eggs are easily prepared in the microwave oven. Cook 6 large eggs in 1.5 litres (6 cups) of water with 50 mL (1/4 cup) vinegar added.

Pour water and vinegar in a dish; cover and bring to a boil by heating at 100% for 10 to 12 minutes.

Break the eggs into a pie plate, being very careful not to break the yolks.

Gently, pour the eggs onto the surface of the boiling water. Carefully prick each yolk and white and cook at 100% for 4 minutes.

Remove the eggs from the water with a skimmer.

Trim the eggs with a knife to form a nice rounded shape.

onto the surface of the boiling water; carefully prick each yolk and white in 2 or 3 places and cook at 100% for 4 minutes.
— With a skimmer, remove

the eggs from the water; trim the eggs with a knife to form a nice rounded shape.
— Place 1 slice of ham on each muffin half.

— Place an egg on each muffin half and cover with one quarter of the hot Hollandaise Sauce before serving.

Eggs Poached in Tomato Sauce

Ingredients
6 large eggs
500 mL (2 cups) tomato sauce

Method
— Place the tomato sauce in a dish and heat at 100% for 7 to 9 minutes or until hot.
— Pour half the hot sauce into a microwave-safe pie plate.
— Break the eggs into the pie plate around the edge, making sure they don't slide into the center of the dish; gently prick each yolk and white in 2 or 3 places with a toothpick.
— Cover the eggs with the remaining sauce.
— Place the plate on a raised rack and cook at 100% for 1 minute.
— Reduce the power to 70% and continue cooking for 4 minutes, giving the plate a half-turn halfway through the cooking time.
— Allow to stand for 5 minutes.

Level of Difficulty	🍴
Preparation Time	5 min
Cost per Serving	$
Number of Servings	6
Nutritional Value	185 calories 7.3 g protein 1.6 mg iron
Food Exchanges	1 oz meat 4 vegetable exchanges
Cooking Time	14 min*
Standing Time	5 min
Power Level	100%, 70%
Write Your Cooking Time Here	

* Cooking time is based on the use of large eggs which are at room temperature when cooking begins.

Eggs Jardinière

Level of Difficulty	🍴🍴
Preparation Time	20 min
Cost per Serving	$
Number of Servings	4
Nutritional Value	291 calories 13.4 g protein 2.8 mg iron
Food Exchanges	2 oz meat 2 vegetable exchanges 2 fat exchanges
Cooking Time	22 min*
Standing Time	None
Power Level	100%
Write Your Cooking Time Here	

* Cooking time is based on the use of large eggs which are at room temperature when cooking begins.

Ingredients
8 large eggs
50 mL (1/4 cup) butter
2 onions, sliced
2 stalks of celery, sliced
1 red pepper, sliced
15 mL (1 tablespoon) parsley
5 mL (1 teaspoon) marjoram
salt and pepper to taste
1.5 litres (6 cups) water
50 mL (1/4 cup) white vinegar

Method
— Put the butter in a dish and add all the vegetables and seasonings; cover and cook at 100% for 4 to 5 minutes or until the vegetables are tender, stirring once, halfway through the cooking time. Set aside.
— Pour the water and vinegar into a dish, cover and bring to the boil by heating at 100% for 10 to 12 minutes.
— Break the eggs into a plate; gently slide the eggs onto the surface of the boiling water; carefully pierce the membrane covering each yolk and white with a toothpick and cook at 100% for 5 minutes.
— With a skimmer, remove the eggs from the water and trim them with a knife in order to from a rounder shape.
— Place the eggs on a serving plate, garnished with the cooked vegetables.

MICROTIPS

For a Succulent Fruit Omelette

An omelette served as a dessert (see page 40) will be a pleasant surprise. As an added bonus, the omelette can be prepared ahead of time and re- heated. If this is the case, sprinkle with the icing sugar just before serving.

Caught Unaware? Never!

Add some tomato, leftover meat or some ham to scrambled eggs. Reheat the ingredients and add them when you are stirring the eggs for the first time. For variety, cook a few slices of bacon for 2 to 4 minutes in the microwave oven; add some mushrooms, diced red or green pepper and continue to cook for 2 minutes. Add this mixture to the eggs before cooking them.

Eggs en Matelote

Level of Difficulty	⑪ ⑪
Preparation Time	20 min
Cost per Serving	$
Number of Servings	4
Nutritional Value	311 calories 13.4 g protein 2.8 mg iron
Food Exchanges	1.5 oz meat 2 vegetable exchanges 1 bread exchange 1-1/2 fat exchanges
Cooking Time	14 min
Standing Time	None
Power Level	100%
Write Your Cooking Time Here	

* Cooking time is based on the use of large eggs which are at room temperature when cooking begins.

Ingredients
4 large eggs, poached (see method for poaching eggs, explained on page 44)
30 mL (2 tablespoons) butter
30 mL (2 tablespoons) mushrooms, sliced
3 onions, chopped
15 mL (1 tablespoon) flour
150 mL (2/3 cup) beef broth
150 mL (2/3 cup) white wine
2 egg yolks
4 slices crusty bread, toasted

Method
— Place the butter, mushrooms and onions in a dish; cover and cook at 100% for 3 minutes, stirring once during the cooking time.
— Sprinkle with the flour and mix well.
— Pour in the broth and wine; cover and cook at 100% for 10 minutes.
— Transfer to a blender; purée at high speed for a few seconds; return to the dish, add the egg yolks and stir well.
— Heat at 100% for 1 minute or until thickened.
— Carefully place a poached egg on each slice of toast and cover with one quarter of the sauce before serving.

This recipe offers an original way of serving poached eggs. These are the ingredients required.

Sprinkle the vegetables with flour after cooking them at 100% for 3 minutes.

Pour the broth and wine into the dish, cover and cook at 100% for 10 minutes.

Scrambled Eggs with Smoked Salmon

Level of Difficulty	🍴
Preparation Time	15 min
Cost per Serving	$ $
Number of Servings	4
Nutritional Value	326 calories 17 g protein 2.7 g fats
Food Exchanges	2.5 oz meat 1 vegetable exchange 1/2 bread exchange 1-1/2 fat exchanges
Cooking Time	10 min*
Standing Time	None
Power Level	100%
Write Your Cooking Time Here	

* Cooking time is based on the use of large eggs which are at room temperature when cooking begins.

Ingredients
7 large eggs
1 red pepper, finely chopped
30 mL (2 tablespoons) butter
90 g (3 oz) smoked salmon, thinly sliced
45 mL (3 tablespoons) 15% cream
salt and pepper to taste
8 7 cm (3 in) wide bread rounds, toasted

Method
— Place the red pepper and butter in a dish; cover and cook at 100% for 3 to 4 minutes.
— Add the smoked salmon; replace the cover and set aside.
— Beat the eggs with a whisk, gradually adding the cream; add salt and pepper to taste, and then add the salmon mixture.
— Cook at 100% for 5 to 6 minutes, stirring after 2 minutes of the cooking time and then stirring once each minute thereafter.
— Divide evenly on top of the toasted bread rounds and serve.

Scrambled Eggs with Smoked Salmon

The subtle combination of these ingredients will please all your guests.

First, in a covered dish, cook the red pepper in the butter.

Add the smoked salmon; replace the cover and set aside.

Beat the eggs with a whisk, gradually adding the cream, seasoning and finally the salmon mixture.

Cook the mixture at 100% for 5 to 6 minutes, stirring after 2 minutes and each minute thereafter.

Place a portion of the cooked mixture on each toasted bread round.

Scrambled Eggs with Rice

Ingredients
8 large eggs
30 mL (2 tablespoons) butter
50 mL (1/4 cup) celery, chopped
50 mL (1/4 cup) green pepper, chopped
125 mL (1/2 cup) 15% cream
50 mL (1/4 cup) white rice, cooked
salt and pepper to taste

Level of Difficulty	🍴
Preparation Time	15 min
Cost per Serving	$
Number of Servings	4
Nutritional Value	274 calories 13.2 g protein 2.3 mg iron
Food Exchanges	2 oz meat 1/2 vegetable exchange 2-1/2 fat exchanges
Cooking Time	13 min*
Standing Time	2 min
Power Level	100%
Write Your Cooking Time Here	

Method
— Place the butter, celery and green pepper in a dish; cover and cook at 100% for 3 to 4 minutes, stirring once during the cooking time; set aside.
— Beat the eggs with a whisk, gradually adding the cream.
— Add the rice, vegetables, salt and pepper.
— Cook at 100% for 7 to 9 minutes, stirring every 2 minutes.
— Allow to stand for 2 minutes before serving.

* Cooking time is based on the use of large eggs which are at room temperature when cooking begins.

Eggs in Ramekins

Level of Difficulty	🍴
Preparation Time	10 min
Cost per Serving	**$**
Number of Servings	4
Nutritional Value	353 calories 18 g protein 3 mg iron
Food Exchanges	2.5 oz meat 1 vegetable exchange 3 fat exchanges
Cooking Time	15 min*
Standing Time	1 min
Power Level	100%, 70%
Write Your Cooking Time Here	

* Cooking time is based on the use of large eggs which are at room temperature when cooking begins.

MICROTIPS

Eggs in Ramekins—Without Ramekins

Not every kitchen has a supply of ramekins at the cook's disposal. No need to worry! Instead of ramekins, place the eggs in a muffin pan that is well greased. However, make sure that the muffin pan is microwave-safe.

Ingredients
8 large eggs
8 slices bacon
125 mL (1/2 cup) mushrooms, thinly sliced
125 mL (1/2 cup) 35% cream
salt and pepper to taste
8 ramekins, greased

Method
— Place the bacon in a dish and cook at 100% for 6 to 8 minutes or until crispy.
— Crumble the bacon into bits and set aside.
— In another dish, cook the mushrooms at 100% for 2 minutes.
— Place an equal amount of crumbled bacon and mushrooms in the bottom of each ramekin.
— Break one egg into each ramekin; gently pierce each yolk and white in 2 or 3 places with a toothpick; top with 15 mL (1 tablespoon) cream and add salt and pepper to taste.
— Place the ramekins on a raised rack in the microwave oven and cook at 70% for 3 to 5 minutes, giving the ramekins a half-turn halfway through the cooking time.
— Let stand for 1 minute.

54

Egg and Salmon Loaf

Level of Difficulty	(icon)
Preparation Time	15 min
Cost per Serving	$
Number of Servings	4
Nutritional Value	248 calories 18 g protein 2.2 mg iron
Food Exchanges	2.5 oz meat 1/2 bread exchange 1/2 fat exchange
Cooking Time	6 min*
Standing Time	3 min
Power Level	70%
Write Your Cooking Time Here	(icon)

* Cooking time is based on the use of large eggs which are at room temperature when cooking begins.

Ingredients
3 large eggs, lightly beaten
1 213 mL (7-1/2 oz) can salmon, drained
250 mL (1 cup) breadcrumbs
50 mL (1/4 cup) 15% cream
125 mL (1/2 cup) celery, diced
30 mL (2 tablespoons) onion, grated
15 mL (1 tablespoon) lemon juice
30 mL (2 tablespoons) parsley

Method
— In a large bowl, place all the ingredients except the parsley and mix well.
— Divide the mixture among 4 greased ramekins and sprinkle the tops with parsley.
— Place the ramekins on a raised rack in the oven and cook at 70% for 4 to 6 minutes, giving them a half-turn halfway through the cooking time.
— Let stand for 3 minutes.

Assemble these few ingredients before preparing this egg and salmon loaf—a dish that is flavorful and easy to make.

After placing the ingredients in a bowl, mix them thoroughly. Beat the eggs in a separate bowl before mixing with the other ingredients.

Place one quarter of the mixture in each of 4 greased ramekins and sprinkle the tops with parsley before placing in the oven.

Give the ramekins a half-turn halfway through the cooking time to ensure uniform cooking.

57

Sauces and Garnishes To Accompany Cooked Omelettes

Parmesan White Sauce

Ingredients
30 mL (2 tablespoons) butter
30 mL (2 tablespoons) flour
250 mL (1 cup) milk
75 mL (1/3 cup) Parmesan cheese, grated
15 mL (1 tablespoon) roasted red pepper, chopped
salt and pepper to taste

Method
— Place the butter in a dish and heat at 100% for 30 seconds to melt it.
— Add the flour and stir to combine.
— Add the milk and cook at 100% for 3 to 4 minutes, stirring twice during cooking.
— Add the Parmesan cheese and red pepper, and season to taste. Mix well.

Velouté Sauce

Ingredients
60 mL (4 tablespoons) butter
1 green onion, sliced
30 mL (2 tablespoons) flour
125 mL (1/2 cup) chicken broth
50 mL (1/4 cup) 15% cream

Method
— Place the butter in a dish and heat at 100% for 1 minute to melt it. Add the green onion and cook at 100% for 1 minute.
— Add the flour and mix well.
— Add the remaining ingredients and stir again to get an even mixture.
— Cook at 100% for 3 to 4 minutes or until the sauce is creamy.

Fish Stock Sauce

Ingredients
30 mL (2 tablespoons) butter
1 leek, finely chopped
30 mL (2 tablespoons) flour
175 mL (3/4 cup) fish stock
45 mL (3 tablespoons) 35% cream

Method
— Place the butter in a dish and heat at 100% for 30 seconds to melt it. Add the leek and cook at 100% for 2 minutes, stirring once.
— Add the flour and mix well.
— Add the other ingredients and mix thoroughly.
— Cook at 100% for 4 to 5 minutes or until the sauce is creamy.

Italian Vegetable Sauce

Ingredients
125 mL (1/2 cup) olive oil
2 medium carrots, grated
2 large onions, finely chopped
2 medium leeks, finely
chopped
1 156 mL (5-1/2 oz) can
tomato paste
1 796 mL (28 oz) can tomatoes
15 mL (1 tablespoon) sugar
5 mL (1 teaspoon) salt
10 mL (2 teaspoons) oregano
10 mL (2 teaspoons) basil

Method
— Pour the oil into a 2 L (8
 cup) container and heat at
 100% for 2 minutes.
— Add the vegetables and the
 remaining ingredients;
 mix well.
— Cover and cook at 100%
 for 14 to 16 minutes, or
 until the sauce has the
 desired texture.

Sauces and Garnishes To Accompany Cooked Omelettes

Spinach Garnish

Ingredients
450 g (1 lb) fresh spinach
pinch of nutmeg
125 mL (1/2 cup) chicken
broth
salt and pepper to taste

Method
— Rinse the spinach
thoroughly under running
water; discard tough
stems and chop.
— Place the spinach in a dish,
cover and cook at 100%
for 5 to 6 minutes, stirring
once.
— Place the cooked spinach
in a blender; add the
remaining ingredients;
purée.
— Reheat the purée at 100%
for 2 minutes.

Mushroom Garnish

Ingredients
450 g (1 lb) mushrooms
30 mL (2 tablespoons) butter
15 mL (1 tablespoon) lemon
juice
30 mL (2 tablespoons) flour
125 mL (1/2 cup) chicken
broth
salt and pepper to taste

Method
— Wipe the mushrooms with
a damp cloth to clean
them and dry with paper
towel.
— Slice the mushrooms
thinly and place in a dish;
add the butter and lemon
juice and cook at 100%
for 4 to 5 minutes, stirring
once during cooking.
— Add the flour and mix
well.
— Stir in the chicken broth
and cook at 100% for 1 to
2 minutes or until the
mixture is thickened.
— Season to taste before
serving.

Green Pea Garnish

Ingredients
450 g (1 lb) frozen green peas
15 mL (1 tablespoon) melted
butter
50 mL (1/4 cup) 35% cream
salt and pepper to taste

Method
— Place the peas in a dish;
cover and cook at 100%
for 7 to 9 minutes, stirring
once during the cooking
time.
— Put the cooked peas in a
blender; purée.
— Force the purée through a
strainer to remove the
skins; add the melted
butter and cream.
— Season to taste and cook at
100% for 2 minutes.

Tomatoes Stuffed with Eggs

Ingredients
4 tomatoes
4 large eggs
salt and pepper to taste
30 mL (2 tablespoons)

Parmesan cheese, grated
15 mL (1 tablespoon) parsley,
chopped

Method
— With a sharp knife, cut off
  the top of each tomato
  and scoop out the pulp.
— Place the tomatoes on a
  plate that is
  microwave-safe and
  season to taste.
— Break an egg into each
  tomato.
— With a toothpick, stir the
  white of the egg and
  pierce the yolk in 2 places.
— Combine the cheese and
  parsley, and sprinkle on
  each tomato.
— Place the plate on a raised
  rack in the oven and cook
  at 70% for 1 to 3 minutes,
  giving the plate a half-
  turn halfway through the
  cooking time.
— Let stand for 2 minutes.

Level of Difficulty	🍴 🍴
Preparation Time	15 min
Cost per Serving	$
Number of Servings	4
Nutritional Value	129 calories 9 g protein 2 mg iron
Food Exchanges	1 oz meat 1-1/2 vegetable exchanges
Cooking Time	3 min*
Standing Time	2 min
Power Level	70%
Write Your Cooking Time Here	

* Cooking time is based on the use of large eggs which are at room
  temperature when cooking begins.

Omelette Parmentier

Level of Difficulty	🍴🍴
Preparation Time	15 min
Cost per Serving	$
Number of Servings	8
Nutritional Value	227 calories 16.1 g protein 2.1 mg iron
Food Exchanges	2 oz meat 2 vegetable exchanges 1/2 fat exchange
Cooking Time	17 min*
Standing Time	2 min
Power Level	100%, 70%
Write Your Cooking Time Here	

* Cooking time is based on the use of large eggs which are at room temperature when cooking begins.

Ingredients
8 large eggs
30 mL (2 tablespoons) butter
250 mL (1 cup) potatoes, grated
125 mL (1/2 cup) carrots, grated
50 mL (1/4 cup) onion, finely chopped
15 mL (1 tablespoon) parsley
salt and pepper to taste
125 mL (1/2 cup) 10% cream
250 mL (1 cup) ham, cut in cubes
125 mL (1/2 cup) orange cheddar cheese, grated

Method
— Place the butter in a dish; add the vegetables and parsley; season to taste.
— Cover and cook at 100% for 4 to 6 minutes, stirring once during the cooking time. Set aside.
— Mix the eggs and cream, season to taste and pour over the vegetables. Top with the ham.
— Place the dish on a raised rack in the oven and cook at 70% for 9 to 10 minutes, giving the dish a half-turn halfway through the cooking time.
— Sprinkle with the grated cheddar cheese and continue to cook at 100% for 1 minute.
— Let stand for 2 minutes.

Assemble these ingredients to produce, in a very short time, a delicious omelette suitable for all occasions.

Combine the butter, potatoes, carrots, onions and parsley, and cook at 100%.

After adding the eggs and cream, place the cubes of ham on top.

63

Scrambled Egg Tartlets

Level of Difficulty	🍴
Preparation Time	10 min
Cost per Serving	$
Number of Servings	4
Nutritional Value	526 calories 16.8 g protein 27.1 mg iron
Food Exchanges	2 oz meat 2 vegetable exchanges 2 bread exchanges 3-1/2 fat exchanges
Cooking Time	12 min*
Standing Time	2 min
Power Level	100%
Write Your Cooking Time Here	

* Cooking time is based on the use of large eggs which are at room
  temperature when cooking begins.

Ingredients
8 tart shells
7 large eggs
30 mL (2 tablespoons) butter
225 g (8 oz) asparagus,
coarsely chopped
50 mL (1/4 cup) cooked ham,
chopped
125 mL (1/2 cup) 35% cream
salt and pepper to taste

Method
— Place the butter in a dish
  and add the asparagus;
  cook at 100% for 5 to 6
  minutes, stirring once
  halfway through the
  cooking time.
— Add the ham, cover and
  set aside.
— Mix the eggs and cream,
  and season to taste.
— Add the asparagus and
  ham to the egg mixture
  and mix well.
— Cook at 100% for 5 to 6
  minutes, stirring once
  after 2 minutes of cooking
  and then once each minute
  until the end of the
  cooking cycle.
— Let stand for 2 minutes.
— Spoon an equal amount of
  the mixture into each tart
  shell and serve.

MICROTIPS

For People on a Diet

To cut down on the number of calories, substitute unsweetened, evaporated milk for the 35% cream called for in recipes. This will not change the taste but will allow you to enjoy these delicious dishes.

Technology to the Rescue

The recipe for scrambled egg tartlets is a perfect one to keep in mind when you must improvise for unexpected guests. All you need is to keep a package of frozen tart shells in the freezer as well as cans of ham and asparagus in the cupboard. With such provisions on hand, and thanks to the microwave, you can produce a first-class dish in a very short time.

Swiss Fondue

Level of Difficulty	🍴
Preparation Time	10 min
Cost per Serving	$
Number of Servings	4
Nutritional Value	349 calories 18.7 g protein 567 mg calcium
Food Exchanges	4 oz meat 1 fat exchange
Cooking Time	5 min
Standing Time	None
Power Level	70%
Write Your Cooking Time Here	

Ingredients
1 clove garlic, cut in half
750 mL (3 cups) Gruyère cheese, grated
30 mL (2 tablespoons) flour
pinch of nutmeg
white pepper to taste
250 mL (1 cup) white wine
30 mL (2 tablespoons) brandy
crusty bread, cut into cubes

Method
— Rub the inside of a deep 2 L (8 cup) dish with the garlic, throw away the garlic.
— Place the grated cheese, flour and seasonings in a plastic bag and shake to flour the cheese.
— Pour the wine and brandy into the prepared dish; heat at 70% for 2 to 3 minutes or until hot.
— Add the cheese to the hot wine and brandy mixture, stirring to mix thoroughly.
— Heat at 70% until the cheese is melted and smooth, stirring every 2 minutes.
— Serve with cubes of crusty bread.

Cheese Ball

Level of Difficulty	🍴🍴
Preparation Time	15 min*
Cost per Serving	$ $
Number of Servings	14
Nutritional Value	241 calories 8.3 g protein 164 mg calcium
Food Exchanges	2 oz meat 2 fat exchanges
Cooking Time	3 min
Standing Time	None
Power Level	100%, 70%
Write Your Cooking Time Here	

* This mixture must be refrigerated for 2 to 3 hours before serving.

Ingredients
15 mL (1 tablespoon) butter
50 mL (1/4 cup) green pepper, finely chopped
50 mL (1/4 cup) green onions, finely chopped
450 g (16 oz) cream cheese
225 g (8 oz) blue cheese
115 g (4 oz) processed cheese spread
15 mL (1 tablespoon) roasted red pepper, chopped
30 mL (2 tablespoons) relish
10 mL (2 teaspoons) Worcestershire sauce
1 clove garlic, crushed
125 mL (1/2 cup) walnuts, finely chopped

Method
— Place the butter in a dish and add the green pepper and green onions; cover and cook at 100% for 1 to 2 minutes; set aside.
— Place the cream cheese in another dish and heat at 70% for 1 minute to soften; add the remaining ingredients except the walnuts.
— Add the cooked vegetables after they have cooked a bit and mix well.
— Refrigerate the mixture for 2 to 3 hours until it becomes firm.
— Shape into a ball and roll in the chopped walnuts.

This cheese ball will really satisfy the munchies. First, assemble all the ingredients required for its preparation.

After refrigerating the cheese mixture, shape it into a ball.

Roll the cheese ball in chopped walnuts.

Camembert Fritters

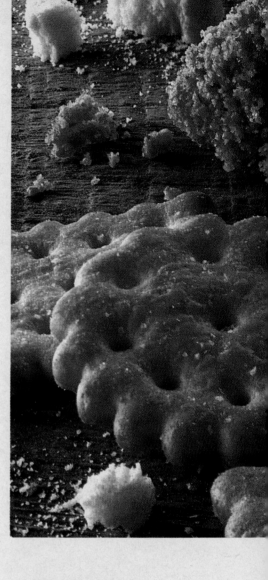

Level of Difficulty	🍴🍴🍴
Preparation Time	20 min*
Cost per Serving	$ $
Number of Servings	6
Nutritional Value	331 calories 18.4 g protein 27 g carbohydrate
Food Exchanges	3 oz meat 1 bread exchange 1/2 fat exchange
Cooking Time	2 min
Standing Time	None
Power Level	100%, 70%
Write Your Cooking Time Here	

* The Camembert should be placed in the freezer for 1 hour before preparing this recipe.

Ingredients
450 g (1 lb) Camembert cheese
30 mL (2 tablespoons) butter
125 mL (1/2 cup) breadcrumbs
2 eggs, beaten
50 mL (1/4 cup) flour

Method
— Cut the Camembert cheese into sixteen equal wedges and freeze for 1 hour.
— Place the butter in a dish and heat at 100% for 30 seconds to melt it; add the breadcrumbs and mix well.
— With a fork, whip the eggs.
— Roll each cheese wedge in the flour, then in the beaten egg and finally in the breadcrumbs.
— Place 8 wedges in a circle on a plate, with the points of the wedges towards the center.
— Heat at 70% for 1 minute.
— Repeat for the remaining 8 wedges.

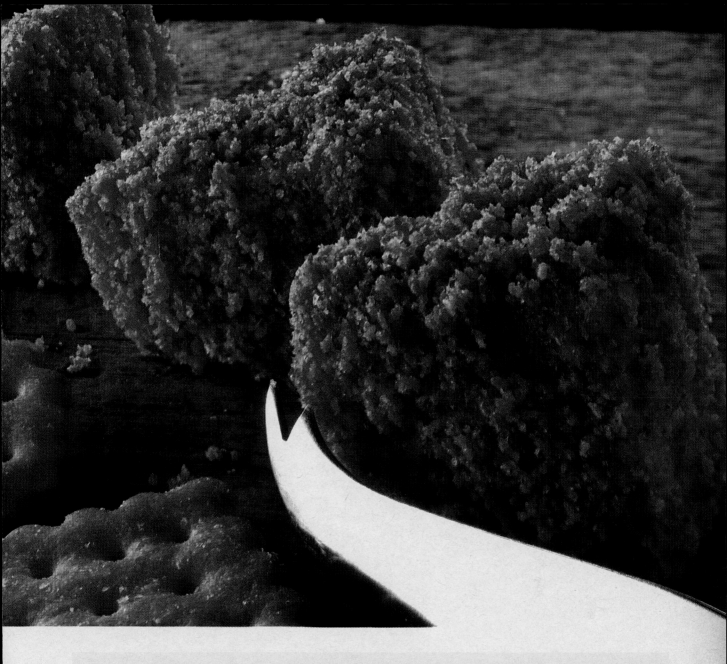

MICROTIPS

A Delicious Crust for Cheesecake

Mix 125 mL (1/2 cup) butter, 325 mL (1-1/3 cup) graham cracker crumbs and 30 mL (2 tablespoons) brown sugar until thoroughly combined. Press into the bottom of a pie plate. Cook on a raised rack at 70% for 3 minutes. Give the plate a half-turn, halfway through the cooking time. Consult *Desserts,* Volume 3, of this series to find variations of this recipe.

What About Brie for Fritters?

Brie and Camembert cheeses are very similar and can easily be substituted one for the other, whatever the recipe. If you don't happen to have any Camembert, Brie will do just as well and your recipe will be just as successful. However, make sure you use a good quality Brie or Camembert, one with a smooth, creamy texture, that does not have a white chalky crust running through it.

Eggplant Parmesan

Level of Difficulty	🍴🍴
Preparation Time	20 min
Cost per Serving	$
Number of Servings	4
Nutritional Value	398 calories 25.9 g protein 652 mg calcium
Food Exchanges	3.5 oz meat 3 vegetable exchanges 1 fat exchange
Cooking Time	12 min
Standing Time	3 min
Power Level	70%
Write Your Cooking Time Here	

* The eggplant must be allowed to stand for 30 minutes so that as much moisture as possible is drawn out before preparing this recipe.

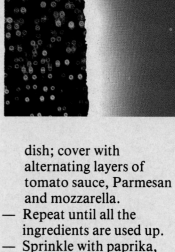

Ingredients
1 large eggplant or 675 g (1-1/2 lbs) eggplant pulp
coarse salt
15 mL (1 tablespoon) basil
125 mL (1/2 cup) Parmesan cheese, grated
375 mL (1-1/2 cups) tomato sauce
225 g (8 oz) mozzarella cheese, thinly sliced
paprika to taste

Method
— Cut the eggplant into very thin slices and sprinkle generously with the coarse salt.
— Let the slices sit for 30 minutes to draw out all the moisture; then rinse under running cold water and dry well.
— Combine the basil and Parmesan cheese.
— Place a layer of eggplant slices in the bottom of a dish; cover with alternating layers of tomato sauce, Parmesan and mozzarella.
— Repeat until all the ingredients are used up.
— Sprinkle with paprika, cover and cook at 70% for 10 to 12 minutes, giving the dish a half-turn halfway through the cooking time.
— Let stand for 3 mintues.

Served either as a side dish or main course, this recipe for eggplant Parmesan will please everyone. First, assemble all the ingredients required for its preparation.

Sprinkle the eggplant slices generously with coarse salt and allow to stand for 30 minutes to draw out the moisture.

Place the eggplant slices in the bottom of a dish and cover with alternating layers of tomato sauce, Parmesan cheese and mozzarella cheese.

Macédoine of Vegetables with Cheese

Level of Difficulty	🍴
Preparation Time	10 min
Cost per Serving	$
Number of Servings	4
Nutritional Value	126 calories 7.9 g protein 0.5 mg iron
Food Exchanges	1 oz meat 2 vegetable exchanges
Cooking Time	9 min
Standing Time	3 min
Power Level	100%
Write Your Cooking Time Here	

Ingredients
125 mL (1/2 cup) broccoli flowerets
125 mL (1/2 cup) cauliflower flowerets
125 mL (1/2 cup) celery, thinly sliced
125 mL (1/2 cup) green onions, chopped
50 mL (1/4 cup) water
4 slices orange cheddar cheese

Method
— Place the vegetables in a dish with the water; cover and cook at 100% for 5 to 7 minutes, stirring once during cooking.
— Let stand for 3 minutes and drain.
— Place the cheese slices on top of the hot vegetables and continue to cook at 100% for 1 to 2 minutes or just until the cheese is melted, giving the dish a half-turn halfway through the cooking time.
— Let stand for 3 minutes.

Cheese Soup

Level of Difficulty	🍴
Preparation Time	20 min
Cost per Serving	$
Number of Servings	4
Nutritional Value	396 calories 18 g protein 473 mg calcium
Food Exchanges	2 oz meat 1 vegetable exchange 1/2 milk exchange 2-1/2 fat exchanges
Cooking Time	15 min
Standing Time	None
Power Level	100%
Write Your Cooking Time Here	

Ingredients
45 mL (3 tablespoons) butter
30 mL (2 tablespoons) almonds, slivered
75 mL (1/3 cup) onion, finely chopped
50 mL (1/4 cup) carrot, grated
50 mL (1/4 cup) flour
375 mL (1-1/2 cups) milk
1 284 mL (10 oz) can chicken consommé, undiluted
salt and pepper to taste
500 mL (2 cups) processed cheese spread
parsley

Method
— Place the butter and almonds in a dish and cook at 100% for 2 to 3 minutes, or until the almonds are a golden color, stirring once during the cooking time.
— Add the onion and carrot and cook at 100% for 2 to 3 minutes, stirring once during cooking.
— Sprinkle with the flour and mix well.
— Add the milk and chicken consommé, and beat with a whisk.
— Cook at 100% for 6 to 8 minutes, or just until the mixture thickens, stirring twice during the cooking time.
— Season to taste, add the processed cheese spread; beat with a whisk to combine.
— Cook at 100% for 1 minute and sprinkle with parsley before serving.

MICROTIPS

Cheese Soup Without Cheese?
It often happens that you get partway through a recipe before realizing that you are short of a main ingredient. Fortunately, substitutions are possible. If, for example, you haven't enough processed cheese for the cheese soup, you can substitute an equal amount of grated cheddar cheese.

Cooking Times for Poached Eggs
Cooking times in the microwave oven vary with the quantities of food to be cooked. Eggs are no exception. In order to poach eggs successfully in the microwave oven, adjust the cooking times as follows:

1 egg . . . . . 45 to 80 seconds

2 eggs . . . . 65 to 95 seconds
4 eggs . . 135 to 195 seconds

An Ideal Utensil: The Tube Pan
The tube pan is perfect for the even cooking of foods. In effect, the microwaves are concentrated away from the center of the oven and therefore away from the center of the dishes used. In a tube pan, there is no food in the center of the pan.

Endive au Gratin

Level of Difficulty	🍴🍴
Preparation Time	15 min
Cost per Serving	**$**
Number of Servings	4
Nutritional Value	309 calories 24.5 g protein 298 mg calcium
Food Exchanges	3.5 oz meat 1 vegetable exchange 1/4 milk exchange 1/2 fat exchange
Cooking Time	12 min
Standing Time	None
Power Level	100%, 70%
Write Your Cooking Time Here	

Ingredients
6 endives
15 mL (1 tablespoon) water
15 mL (1 tablespoon) lemon juice
12 slices cooked ham

Cheddar Sauce:
375 mL (1-1/2 cup) cheddar cheese, grated
30 mL (2 tablespoons) butter
30 mL (2 tablespoons) flour
250 mL (1 cup) milk
salt and pepper to taste

Method
— First prepare the sauce: put the butter in a dish and heat at 100% for 30 seconds to melt it.
— Add the flour and mix well.
— Add the milk and beat with a whisk.
— Cook at 100% for 3 to 4 minutes, stirring twice during the cooking time.
— Add the cheese and whisk again until it is completely melted.
— Season to taste and set aside.
— Cut each endive in half.
— Mix the water and lemon juice.
— Place the endive in a dish and add the water and lemon juice mixture.
— Cover and cook at 100% for 4 minutes or until the endive is cooked but still crisp.
— Drain and roll a slice of ham around each endive half.
— Cover with the cheese sauce and reheat at 70% for 3 minutes before serving.

Whether served as a side dish or a main dish, endive au gratin is guaranteed to please. Assemble all the required ingredients before starting.

Place the endive in a dish and add the water and lemon juice mixture.

Roll a slice of ham around each endive half and reheat the roll-ups.

Seafood en Coquille

Level of Difficulty	🍴
Preparation Time	20 min
Cost per Serving	$ $ $
Number of Servings	6
Nutritional Value	383 calories 31.2 g protein 3.1 mg iron
Food Exchanges	3.5 oz meat 1 vegetable exchange 2 fat exchanges
Cooking Time	15 min
Standing Time	None
Power Level	100%, 70%
Write Your Cooking Time Here	

Ingredients
225 g (8 oz) cooked scallops
150 g (5 oz) cooked lobster meat
150 g (5 oz) cooked shrimp
75 mL (5 tablespoons) butter
250 mL (1 cup) mushrooms, thinly sliced
50 mL (1/4 cup) celery, thinly sliced
50 mL (1/4 cup) green onions, thinly sliced
50 mL (1/4 cup) white wine
2 egg yolks
salt and pepper to taste

375 mL (1-1/2 cups) soft cheese, such as Saint-Paulin or Oka, grated
paprika to taste

Béchamel Sauce:
45 mL (3 tablespoons) butter
45 mL (3 tablespoons) flour
500 mL (2 cups) milk

Method
— Place the butter in a dish and add the mushrooms, celery and green onions. Cover and cook at 100% for 3 minutes, stirring once during the cooking time.
— Add the wine and all the seafood; cover and set aside.
— To prepare the béchamel sauce: in another dish melt the butter at 100% for 45 seconds; add the flour and mix well.

— Add the milk and beat with a whisk.
— Cook at 100% for 5 to 7 minutes, whisking every 2 minutes.
— Add 30 mL (2 tablespoons) béchamel sauce to the egg yolks and mix this into the remaining béchamel sauce.
— Season to taste and pour the béchamel sauce over the vegetable and seafood mixture which has been equally divided among 6 coquille shells; sprinkle the cheese over the surface of each and top with paprika.
— Cook at 70% for 3 to 4 minutes, giving the coquilles a half-turn halfway through the cooking time.

Divide the seafood and vegetable mixture among six coquille shells. Pour on the béchamel sauce. Top with grated cheese and paprika.

Macaroni and Cheese

Level of Difficulty	
Preparation Time	20 min
Cost per Serving	$
Number of Servings	6
Nutritional Value	382 calories 14.6 g protein 229 mg calcium
Food Exchanges	1.5 oz meat 1 vegetable exchange 2 bread exchanges 2 fat exchanges
Cooking Time	25 min
Standing Time	None
Power Level	100%
Write Your Cooking Time Here	

Ingredients

225 g (8 oz) elbow macaroni
1.5 L (6 cups) boiling water
5 mL (1 teaspoon) salt
5 mL (1 teaspoon) oil
125 mL (1/2 cup) green pepper, chopped
125 mL (1/2 cup) red pepper, chopped
375 mL (1-1/2 cups) orange cheddar cheese, grated
125 mL (1/2 cup) breadcrumbs

Tomato Béchamel Sauce:
50 mL (1/4 cup) butter
50 mL (1/4 cup) flour
375 mL (1-1/2 cups) milk
375 mL (1-1/2 cups) tomato juice

Method

— Place the elbow macaroni in boiling water along with the salt and oil; cover and cook at 100% for 5 to 7 minutes, or until the pasta is cooked to your taste, stirring twice during the cooking time. Drain and set aside.
— Place the peppers in a dish, add 30 mL (2 tablespoons) water; cover and cook at 100% for 3 to 4 minutes. Stir once.
— Drain the peppers and add to the macaroni; set aside.
— To prepare the tomato béchamel sauce: melt the butter at 100% for 45 seconds in another dish; add the flour and mix well.
— Add the milk and beat with a whisk; add the tomato juice and mix well.
— Cook at 100% for 7 to 9 minutes, stirring twice during the cooking time.
— Add 250 mL (1 cup) of the grated cheddar cheese to the sauce and beat with a whisk until the cheese is melted.
— Pour over the macaroni.

— In another bowl, mix the remaining cheddar with the breadcrumbs and sprinkle over the macaroni.
— Cook at 100% for 2 to 4 minutes, giving the dish a half-turn halfway through the cooking time.

MICROTIPS

A Substitute
If orange cheddar cheese is unavailable, you can readily substitute white cheddar cheese. Both have the same taste and the same nutrients; the color added to orange cheddar simply gives your dishes a touch of color.

A Budget Idea
There is no need to buy commercially prepared breadcrumbs if you own a blender. Simply save the left-over heels of bread and let them dry out. Then, you can run them through the electric blender for a few minutes. Nothing wasted in your kitchen!

The Combination of Eggs and Cheese

Quiches, omelettes, soufflés, flans, casseroles—cooks through the centuries have explored the possibilities of egg and cheese combinations. Quiches originated in German cuisine, where the word "kuchen" meant "cake." The best known, certainly, is Quiche Lorraine which contains bacon bits and Gruyère cheese. But the variations are innumerable simply because quiche recipes adapt very easily to the contents of your refrigerator. A recipe for a broccoli and cheese quiche is really tempting, but all you can find is spinach in your freezer? No problem; substitutions are permitted. And if you get the urge to add a little color by adding bits of red or green pepper—go for it!

The recipes for omelettes and cheese soufflés are equally adaptable. If you are prepared to accept a slight change in taste, you can replace Gruyère with cheddar or another hard cheese. This same substitution can be applied in the recipes for seafood coquilles where you can use Saint-Paulin, Port-Salut or some Oka according to your taste or what you have on hand.

Broccoli and Cheese Quiche

Level of Difficulty	🍴
Preparation Time	10 min*
Cost per Serving	$
Number of Servings	6
Nutritional Value	361 calories 20.9 g protein 431 mg iron
Food Exchanges	2.5 oz meat 1 vegetable exchange 1 bread exchange 1-1/2 fat exchanges
Cooking Time	25 min
Standing Time	5 min
Power Level	100%, 50%
Write Your Cooking Time Here	

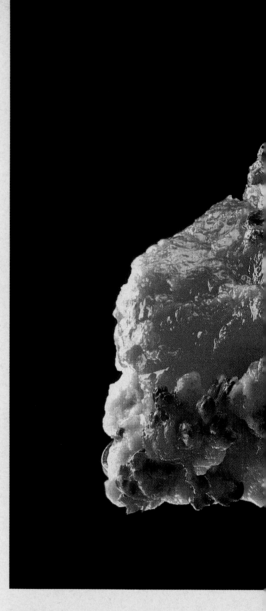

* This dish must stand for 1 hour before the final cooking.

Ingredients
1 284 g (10 oz) package frozen, chopped broccoli
500 mL (2 cups) orange cheddar cheese, grated
6 slices of bread, cut into cubes
6 large eggs
15 mL (1 tablespoon) flour
375 mL (1-1/2 cups) milk
5 mL (1 teaspoon) oregano
salt and pepper to taste

Method
— Remove the broccoli from the package and place in a dish; cover and cook at 100% for 4 to 5 minutes.
— Drain and set aside.
— Place the cubes of bread in a 22.5 cm (9 inch) round dish and add broccoli.
— Beat the eggs and flour in a bowl; add the milk and seasonings. Pour over the broccoli.
— Sprinkle with the cheddar cheese, cover and set aside for 1 hour.
— Uncover and place the pan on a raised rack in the oven; cook at 50% for 16 to 20 minutes, giving the dish a half-turn halfway through the cooking time.
— Cover and let stand for 5 minutes before serving.

MICROTIPS

How To Tell If a Quiche Is Cooked

The quiche is cooked when a knife inserted in the center comes out coated with half-cooked egg mixture. Allow the quiche to stand, covered, for 5 minutes to finish cooking.

Instant Dips

When making a dip with cream cheese, soften the cheese by removing it from its packaging of aluminum foil and heat at 30% for one minute.

To Keep a Fondue Very Hot

If the fondue cools while on the table, return it to the microwave oven for a few seconds. Make sure, however, that your fondue pot is safe to use in a microwave.

Crab Quiche

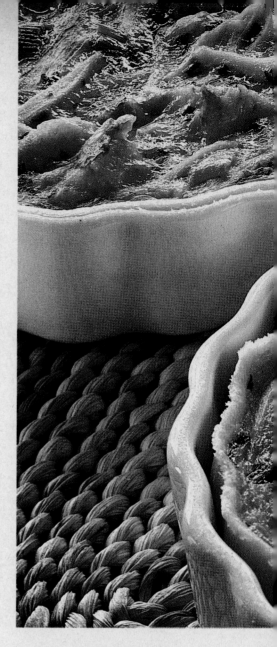

Level of Difficulty	🍴
Preparation Time	15 min
Cost per Serving	$ $
Number of Servings	6
Nutritional Value	304 calories 14.5 g protein 112.4 mg calcium
Food Exchanges	2 oz meat 1 bread exchange 2 fat exchanges
Cooking Time	17 min
Standing Time	5 min
Power Level	100%, 70%
Write Your Cooking Time Here	

Ingredients
300 mL (1-1/4 cups) cooked snow crabmeat
1 pie crust
30 mL (2 tablespoons) butter
3 green onions, chopped
30 mL (2 tablespoons) parsley
salt and pepper to taste
30 mL (2 tablespoons) white vermouth
3 large eggs
250 mL (1 cup) 10% cream
15 mL (1 tablespoon) tomato paste
50 mL (1/4 cup) Gruyère cheese, grated
paprika to taste

Method
— Place the butter, green onions and parsley in a dish; cook at 100% for 2 to 3 minutes.
— Add the crabmeat; season to taste.
— Add the vermouth and mix well; cook at 100% for 1 to 1-1/2 minutes and set aside.
— Add the cream to the eggs and whisk; add the tomato paste and pour over the vegetable and crab mixture. Stir to combine.
— Pour into the pie crust; sprinkle with the Gruyère and paprika.
— Place the pie plate on a raised rack in the oven and cook at 70% for 10 to 12 minutes, giving the plate a half-turn halfway through the cooking time.
— Let stand for 5 minutes before serving.

Once you've assembled all the ingredients, the crab quiche can be prepared in a very short time.

Add the crabmeat to the cooked mixture of green onions and parsley.

Pour the egg mixture into the crust and sprinkle with Gruyère and paprika.

Pizza Soufflé

Level of Difficulty	🍴
Preparation Time	20 min
Cost per Serving	$
Number of Servings	8
Nutritional Value	389 calories 24.8 g protein 535 mg calcium
Food Exchanges	3 oz meat 2 vegetable exchanges 1 bread exchange 1/4 milk exchange
Cooking Time	15 min
Standing Time	5 min
Power Level	70%
Write Your Cooking Time Here	

Ingredients
450 g (1 lb) mozzarella cheese
8 slices bread, torn into soft crumbs
250 mL (1 cup) milk
15 mL (1 tablespoon) oregano
375 mL (1-1/2 cups) tomato sauce
6 large eggs
50 mL (1/4 cup) Parmesan cheese, grated
paprika to taste

Method
— Cut the mozzarella into thin slices.
— Soak the breadcrumbs in the milk.
— Add the oregano to the tomato sauce.
— Place the soaked breadcrumbs in the bottom of a dish and cover with alternating layers of tomato sauce and mozzarella.
— In a bowl, beat the eggs and add the Parmesan; pour over the layers in the dish.
— Sprinkle with paprika; place the dish on a raised rack in the oven and cook at 70% for 12 to 15 minutes, giving the dish a half-turn halfway through the cooking time.

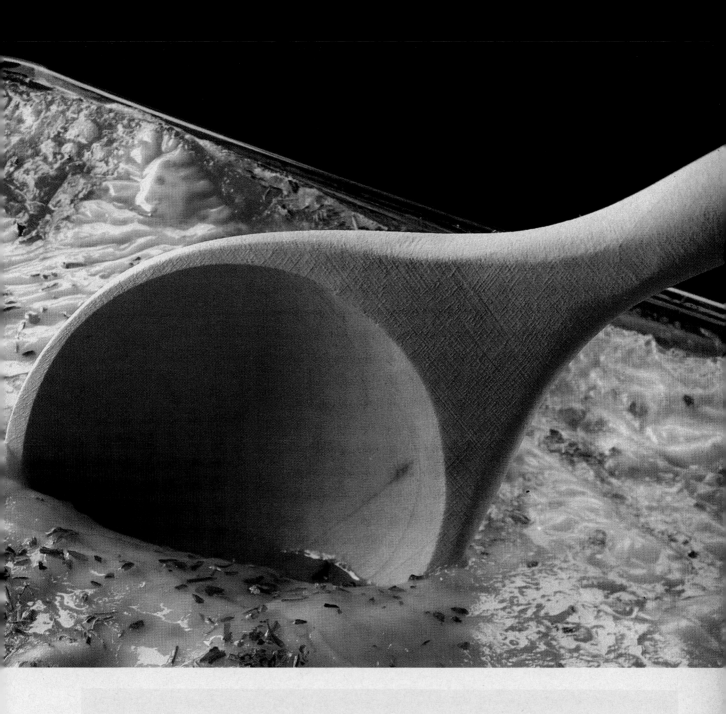

MICROTIPS

A Pizza Without Dough

The pizza soufflé is a good choice for dieters since it contains only 389 calories. You can reduce the calories further by replacing the milk with a mixture of half milk, half water or by using skim-milk mozzarella.

Would you like to lower the calories count even futher? Make a pizza without a crust! Omit the breadcrumbs used in our pizza soufflé recipe. Make sure, though, that the dish is well greased and that you use a thick layer of tomato sauce in the bottom.

Cheese and Tomato Flan

Level of Difficulty	🍴🍴
Preparation Time	20 min
Cost per Serving	$
Number of Servings	6
Nutritional Value	240 calories 6.5 g protein 10.3 mg iron
Food Exchanges	1 oz meat 1 bread exchange 2 fat exchanges
Cooking Time	18 min
Standing Time	5 min
Power Level	70%
Write Your Cooking Time Here	

Ingredients
1 25 cm (10 inch) round pie dough
45 mL (3 tablespoons) capers, chopped
75 mL (1/3 cup) Gruyère cheese, grated
250 mL (1 cup) tomatoes, peeled and chopped
2 large eggs, beaten
50 mL (1/4 cup) milk
125 mL (1/2 cup) 35% cream
salt and pepper to taste
paprika to taste

Method
— Place the pie dough in a flan pan and prick all over with a fork.
— Place on a raised rack in the oven and cook at 70% for 5 to 6 minutes giving the pan a half-turn halfway through the cooking time.
— Spread the capers over the bottom of the crust and cover with the Gruyère and tomatoes; set aside.
— In a bowl, mix the beaten eggs, milk and cream; combine thoroughly; season to taste and pour into the crust.
— Sprinkle with paprika; place on a raised rack in the oven; cook at 70% for 10 to 12 minutes, giving the pan a half-turn halfway through the cooking time.
— Allow to stand for 5 minutes.

MICROTIPS

How To Cook Flans Evenly

Whenever possible, grate the cheese for use in cooking: it will cook faster and more evenly. As well, you are not as likely to overcook the other ingredients.

Higher Is Better!

Our recipes frequently specify that dishes should be cooked on a raised rack. This positioning of your dish will ensure that it is cooked evenly, since the microwaves can thus

reach the bottom of the dish. If your oven does not have a removable rack, purchase one. Most microwave accessory departments or shops will carry several models.

Vegetables au Gratin

Level of Difficulty	
Preparation Time	20 min
Cost per Serving	$
Number of Servings	4
Nutritional Value	267 calories 9.6 g protein 376 mg calcium
Food Exchanges	1 oz meat 1 vegetable exchange 1/2 bread exchange 3 fat exchanges
Cooking Time	14 min
Standing Time	3 min
Power Level	100%
Write Your Cooking Time Here	

Ingredients
1 small onion, diced
3 medium carrots, diced
1 medium potato, diced
2 medium slices rutabaga, diced
50 mL (1/4 cup) water
85 g (3 oz) Gruyère cheese, grated
paprika to taste
salt and pepper to taste
2 mL (1/2 teaspoon) nutmeg
125 mL (1/2 cup) fine breadcrumbs

Velouté Sauce:
30 mL (2 tablespoons) butter
30 mL (2 tablespoons) flour
30 mL (2 tablespoons) 35% cream
salt and pepper to taste
2 mL (1/2 teaspoon) nutmeg
250 mL (1 cup) chicken broth

Method
— To prepare the velouté sauce, put the butter in a dish and heat at 100% for 30 seconds.
— Add the flour and mix well.
— Using a whisk, beat in the cream and season to taste.
— Pour in the chicken broth, mix and cook at 100% for 4 to 5 minutes or until the mixture is thickened, stirring twice during the

cooking time; set aside.
— Place all the vegetables in a dish, add the water; cover and cook at 100% for 4 to 5 minutes, until the vegetables are cooked but still crisp, stirring once halfway through the cooking time.
— Drain and set the cooking juices aside.
— Sprinkle half the Gruyère cheese over the cooked vegetables and stir to mix

well; season to taste and add the nutmeg.
— Pour the reserved velouté sauce in an "au gratin" dish, add the vegetables and their cooking juices.
— Cook at 100% for 2 to 3 minutes.
— Top with the remaining Gruyère and sprinkle with the breadcrumbs.
— Cover and let stand for 3 minutes before serving.

This recipe for vegetables au gratin is suitable for any occasion. These are the ingredients required to prepare this dish.

Cheese and Rice Loaf

Level of Difficulty	🍴
Preparation Time	10 min
Cost per Serving	$
Number of Servings	4
Nutritional Value	440 calories 14.3 g protein 232 mg calcium
Food Exchanges	2.5 oz meat 1 vegetable exchange 1 bread exchange 3 fat exchanges
Cooking Time	6 min
Standing Time	3 min
Power Level	70%
Write Your Cooking Time Here	

Ingredients
3 large eggs
60 mL (4 tablespoons) oil
5 mL (1 teaspoon) basil
30 mL (2 tablespoons) parsley
250 (1 cup) strong cheddar cheese, grated
375 mL (1-1/2 cups) white rice, cooked
125 mL (1/2 cup) chili sauce
50 mL (1/4 cup) walnuts, chopped

Method
— In a bowl, beat the eggs, then add the oil and basil.
— Mix in the parsley, cheddar and rice; combine thoroughly.
— Pour this mixture into a loaf pan and press lightly on the surface to spread evenly.
— Combine the chili sauce and walnuts; pour over the mixture in the pan.
— Cover both ends of the pan with strips of aluminum foil.
— Place on a raised rack in the oven and cook at 70% for 4 to 6 minutes; halfway through the cooking time, remove the aluminum foil and give the pan a half-turn.
— Cover and let stand for 3 minutes before serving.

MICROTIPS

Aluminum Foil: An Invaluable Tool

In the microwave oven, the cooking is always more intense at the edges of a dish than in the center. Because of this, when using a rectangular shaped container, you may find the food at the ends cooks too much, while the food in the center is undercooked. This is where aluminum foil comes to the rescue; since it is metallic, it blocks the microwaves and protects the food shielded in this way; the food covered by the foil is cooked by heat conduction. For example, by covering the ends of the loaf pan in the recipe for the cheese and rice loaf, you make sure the center of the dish will be cooked properly, at the same speed as the end portions.

Mini-Pizzas

Level of Difficulty	🍴
Preparation Time	15 min
Cost per Serving	$
Number of Servings	4
Nutritional Value	393 calories 20 g protein 436 mg calcium
Food Exchanges	2 oz meat 1 vegetable exchange 2 bread exchanges 1 fat exchange
Cooking Time	4 min
Standing Time	None
Power Level	100%
Write Your Cooking Time Here	

Ingredients
4 English muffins, cut in half, toasted

Garnish:
paprika
250 mL (1 cup) mozzarella cheese, grated
125 mL (1/2 cup) cheddar cheese, grated
125 mL (1/2 cup) pepperoni, finely chopped
30 mL (2 tablespoons) onion, finely chopped
15 mL (1 tablespoon) Parmesan cheese, grated
pinch crushed chili peppers
125 mL (1/2 cup) tomato sauce

Method
— In a bowl, combine all the ingredients for the garnish except the paprika and mozzarella cheese, and mix well.
— Spread an equal amount of the mixture on each muffin half; sprinkle with paprika and mozzarella.
— Place 4 muffin halves in the oven and heat at 100% for 1 to 2 minutes.
— Repeat for the remaining muffin halves.

Hot Snack

Level of Difficulty	🍴
Preparation Time	10 min
Cost per Serving	$
Number of Servings	4
Nutritional Value	486 calories 32.5 g protein 484 mg calcium
Food Exchanges	4 oz meat 1 vegetable exchange 2 bread exchanges
Cooking Time	4 min
Standing Time	None
Power Level	100%
Write Your Cooking Time Here	

Ingredients
4 English muffins, cut in half and toasted
30 mL (2 tablespoons) Dijon mustard
8 slices Black Forest ham
8 slices Emmenthal cheese
8 slices tomato
parsley, chopped

Method
— Spread each muffin half with the Dijon mustard.
— Place the following on each muffin half: one slice of ham, then one slice of cheese and one slice of tomato, and finally sprinkle with parsley.
— Place 4 muffin halves in the oven and heat at 100% for 1 to 2 minutes.
— Repeat for the remaining muffin halves.

Delicious Dips

While you're waiting for tardy friends to arrive for a dinner party, satisfy your more punctual guests with a snack before dinner. A dip, in the middle of a large platter surrounded by raw vegetables, promotes conversation and sharpens the appetite. Whether they are as hungry as wolves or have the appetites of birds, guests can help themselves, as they please. Furthermore, dips have another advantage. They can be prepared well ahead of time—always ready for unexpected company!

Most frequently, the base for these smooth, thick sauces is cream cheese, yoghurt or cream. They adapt very easily to the preferences of each and everyone. Carrot and celery sticks, strips of pepper, cauliflower flowerets and cucumber slices are the usual vegetables served with a dip but you can certainly add to the list such items as mushrooms, broccoli, chunks of rutabaga and anything else that takes your fancy. Try feeding raw vegetables with dips to the children: they'll love them!

MICROTIPS

Hurrah for Substitutes!
The magic of cooking lies in the fact that it lends itself very well to the use of substitutes. You won't, for instance, need to run to the store if you find at the last minute, that you've run out of chili sauce. You can replace it, in your recipe, with an equivalent amount of ordinary ketchup, to which has been added 2 drops of Tabasco sauce.

Rosy Dip

Ingredients
250 mL (1 cup) mayonnaise
125 mL (1/2 cup) chili sauce
125 mL (1/2 cup) celery,
finely chopped
3 green onions, finely
chopped
juice of 1 lemon
2 hard-cooked eggs, thinly
sliced

Method
— Combine all the
  ingredients, except the
  eggs.
— Pour into a serving bowl.
— Cover the dip completely
  with egg slices.
  Refrigerate until ready to
  serve.

Olive Dip

Ingredients
250 mL (1 cup) cream cheese
50 mL (1/4 cup) stuffed
olives, finely chopped
15 mL (1 tablespoon) celery,
finely chopped
15 mL (1 tablespoon) green
pepper, finely chopped
15 mL (1 tablespoon) chives,
finely chopped

Method
— Combine all the
  ingredients well.

Lobster Dip

Ingredients
115 g (4 oz) cream cheese
50 mL (1/4 cup) soft butter
5 mL (1 teaspoon) tarragon
85 g (3 oz) lobster paste
15 mL (1 tablespoon) cognac

Method
— Combine the ingredients
  thoroughly using an
  electric mixer.

MICROTIPS

To Freeze and Defrost Cheese

Grated cheese freezes very well. When freezing slices of cheese, you must make sure they are at least 2 cm (1 inch) thick, otherwise they will crumble when defrosted. For best results, do not freeze cheese for any longer than 3 months. Allow it to defrost slowly by placing in the refrigerator. Cheese that has been frozen will retain its flavor and its nutritional value but its texture may become crumbly. Because of this tendency, cheese that has been frozen is best used in cooking rather than served on a platter of cheeses. Plastic bags that seal, developed especially for the freezer are excellent for freezing cheese. If, for reasons of economy, you wish to re-use the bags, you need only wash them and make sure they are perfectly dry. They can be re-used as long as they are airtight and watertight, even when filled to the brim with water.

Egg and Cheese Terminology

Like all great arts, cooking, in the course of its long history, has developed its own specialized vocabulary. These special terms are used to identify techniques and different dishes or containers. Since you will come across many of these in this volume, we felt it might be useful to provide a list of the most common terms.

Au gratin: To cover a dish with grated cheese and breadcrumbs and brown in the oven to achieve a light golden crust on top.

Beat (egg whites): To incorporate air into the egg whites until they are foamy and stand in soft or stiff peaks, as indicated by the recipe.

Béchamel: A white sauce made with cream or milk in which a roux is used as a thickening agent. It is flavored with onions, salt, pepper, nutmeg and/or bay leaves, depending on the recipe used.

Bind: To thicken a sauce or a soup by adding flour, kneaded butter or eggs.

Blender: A kitchen appliance used primarily to mix foods or to purée them.

Bouquet garni: A small bunch of herbs tied together, used to flavor soups and stews during cooking. The herbs usually consist of parsley, thyme and bay leaves.

Candle: A method of examining eggs either by natural or artificial light to determine their quality.

Eyes: Holes of varying size, found in such cheeses as Emmenthal or Gruyère.

Flambé: To pour spirits over a food and set it alight.

Lardoon: Small strips of pork fat added to certain dishes.

Matelote: A sauce made with red wine and onions to accompany egg dishes.

Mimosa eggs: A garnish for hors d'oeuvres that consists of finely grated hard-boiled eggs.

Poach: To cook eggs in a simmering liquid without their shells.

Ramekin: Small heat-proof container in which an individual serving of various meat or egg dishes is cooked. The word also refers to the food cooked in such dishes as well as to meat and / or cheese tarts.

Room temperature: 22°C or 72°F.

Skim: To remove scum or floating substances such as fat from the surface of cooked food.

Sprinkle: Cover with a light coating of a powdery substance such as Parmesan cheese, breadcrumbs or icing sugar.

Whip: To beat a substance vigorously, with a whisk, egg beater or an electric mixer, in order to incorporate air and make it thick and fluffy.

Culinary Terms

Have you ever been given a menu and found that you were unable to understand many of the words? Not only are there a number of culinary terms that are obscure but there are many ways to cook eggs or cheese that have special terms to describe them. Here is a short glossary of terms with descriptions of their meanings that may help you.

Croque Monsieur: A hot open-faced sandwich made with toasted bread, ham and cheese.

Eggs à la coque: Whole eggs cooked in boiling water for a few minutes.

Eggs Benedict: Eggs placed on a muffin or piece of toast with a slice of cooked ham and Hollandaise Sauce.

Flan: A custard-type tart based on milk, eggs and flour and cooked in the oven.

Florentine: Served with spinach.

Looking-glass eggs: Eggs cooked without mixing the yolk and the whites. These may be fried or baked. In the latter case they are also called "shirred eggs."

Macédoine: A mixture of fruits or vegetables served as a salad or cocktail in a jellied dessert or used in a sauce or as a garnish.

Marbled: Term used to describe cheeses that have small streaks of green or blue mold running through them.

Mornay sauce: A béchamel sauce with cheese added.

Quiche: From the German "kuchen" for cake, a pie with a creamy egg filling.

Sabayon: A warm creamy sauce or pudding consisting of egg yolks, sugar, wine and flavorings.

Soufflé: A dish made principally of eggs that rises as it cooks.

Swiss fondue: A dish consisting of melted cheeses and white wine into which cubes of bread are dipped.

Velouté: A sauce thickened with eggs and cream.

Conversion Chart

Conversion Chart for the Main Measures Used in Cooking

Volume
1 teaspoon............ 5 mL
1 tablespoon......... 15 mL

1 quart (4 cups)....... 1 litre
1 pint (2 cups)....... 500 mL
1/2 cup............ 125 mL
1/4 cup............. 50 mL

Weight
2.2 lb.......... 1 kg (1000 g)
1.1 lb............... 500 g
0.5 lb............... 225 g
0.25 lb.............. 115 g

1 oz................. 30 g

Metric Equivalents for Cooking Temperatures

49°C	120°F	120°C	250°F
54°C	130°F	135°C	275°F
60°C	140°F	150°C	300°F
66°C	150°F	160°C	325°F
71°C	160°F	180°C	350°F
77°C	170°F	190°C	375°F
82°C	180°F	200°C	400°F
93°C	200°F	220°C	425°F
107°C	225°F	230°C	450°F

Readers will note that, in the recipes, we give 250 mL as the equivalent for 1 cup and 450 g as the equivalent for 1 lb and that fractions of these measurements are even less mathematically accurate. The reason for this is that mathematically accurate conversions are just not practical in cooking. Your kitchen scales are simply not accurate enough to weigh 454 g—the true equivalent of 1 lb—and it would be a waste of time to try. The conversions given in this series, therefore, necessarily represent approximate equivalents, but they will still give excellent results in the kitchen. No problems should be encountered if you adhere to either metric or imperial measurements throughout a recipe.

Index